MERRY, *Merry* CHRISTMASES

MERRY, Merry CHRISTMASES

ELAINE CANNON

GRAPHICS BY CARLA CANNON

BOOKCRAFT
SALT LAKE CITY, UTAH

Library of Congress Catalog Card Number: 88-72060

ISBN 0-88494-673-8

First Printing, 1988

Printed in the United States of America

Contents

Preface

Merry, merry Christmases,
friendships,
great accumulation
of cheerful recollections,
affection on earth,
and Heaven at last
for all of us.

So said Charles Dickens. And so we say in love:
Merry, merry Christmases!

And may we all be able to feel that way by the time the preparations of house and heart have been accomplished.

May this be the year that when we call out "Merry Christmas! Happy holidays!" to our friends, loved ones, and helpful strangers, we'll know for sure that Christmas is coming to pass.

This book is to remind you, to awaken you, and to enhance all of the aspects of your holiday. To help you have the merriest Christmas ever. Wasn't it Confucius who said, "Words are the voice of the heart"? May the quotes and the collections in this book prepare the way for a hearty season. May the personal experiences shared herein bring forth delightful recollections of your own.

This book calls to mind the sacred mark of the season, the glad tidings and the wholesome traditions of the holidays. May the suggestions in this book help you rise to the grand occasion of a shining season. May they encourage you to be joyful and triumphant.

Such reading can help you remember that remembering is one of the best spin-offs from celebrating Christmas. Remembrance, like a candle, burns brightest at Christmas. It is a fine seasoning for joy.

It is very appropriate that for most of the Christian world Christmas is celebrated in the midst of winter, when dear people unselfishly work to lighten the dark, drab December. During other seasons nature's beauty lends the charm to our days. But midwinter needs a celebration. So on a dismal day you set the stage for happiness with lights, greens, colors, shimmering delights, art, and quaint expressions of the season everywhere.

A symbol of Christmas—a tune, a fragrance, a treat, a game, a way of giving or opening gifts—suggests a life packed full. Traditions become more precious as the years march along. We reflect upon childhood, upon valued relationships, upon kindnesses given and taken, and upon the stretching wonder of the birth night of Jesus, our Lord and Savior.

John Ruskin suggested: "Make yourselves nests of pleasant thoughts. Yet none of us yet know, for none of us have been taught in early youth, what fairy palaces we may build of beautiful thought—proof against all adversity. Bright fancies, satisfied memories, noble histories, faithful sayings, treasure-houses of precious and restful thoughts, which care cannot disturb, no pain make gloomy, nor poverty take away from us—houses built without hands, for our souls to live in."

This book can help you think back for a moment to other times, other Christmases, back to the fragrance of Christmas in your family home. You can almost smell the savory, spicy, sweet scents your family liked best. You can almost hear the rustlings of Santa at work—the squeaks of the floor, the rattles and the rustles, the faint cries of a talking doll, the bell of a toy train, the distant tinkle of a music box set free for a moment.

With increasing clarity, as you remember, you can almost hear again the new album from Santa pealing from your own record player; hear again your own little ones caroling long ago on the family program; hear again the grand effort of the ward choir tackling *The Messiah!*

And if you lean a little into your listening, you may even hear back far enough to catch the lilt of your own harmony in senior choir when *you* sang about the shepherds on that silent night, that holy night we celebrate. Remember how in one singing, one night suddenly it was Christmas?

Think back to the very real feel of comforting, love-instilling arms around you — of your father, of your grandmother, of someone you loved very much and love yet, even if they are long gone. Reach toward the Lord and his comfort, for it was Jesus who said, "I will encircle thee in the arms of my love. Behold, I am Jesus Christ." (D&C 6:21–21.) Imagine that!

And if for some sad reason at this particular time all is not at its best in life, remember that because of Jesus the greeting of Christmas comes with a promise of ultimate joy. Merry, merry Christmases, always and forever.

1

The Innkeeper's Wife

And she brought forth her firstborn son, and . . . laid him in a manger; because there was no room for them in the inn.

—Luke 2:7

1

The Innkeeper's Wife

You know the story of the first Christmas. Though it happened two thousand years ago, you know the characters of the tender drama. There was the Holy Family—Mary and Joseph, and Jesus, a newborn babe. There were the wise men, and the shepherds who watched over their flocks even by night. And there were herald angels who caroled the glad tidings.

Scriptural accounts are sketchy and are recorded piecemeal in various books. Even with careful study the particulars of that sacred occasion aren't exactly clear. As a woman I have wondered *how* it was accomplished that Mary brought forth her firstborn son. And I have pondered this in my heart.

Suppose there were someone else in the story! Suppose . . .

The coral silk swathed about Lydia's head made her look ruddy and girlish in the glow of the anteroom. A towel girded her to protect her best robes and veils from soil as she moved about putting things in order after the reunions and feastings among their lodgers who were in town for Passover.

All that remained was to snuff out the lights. It was a magic moment. It was then that the lamps seemed to burn brighter, as if they had a life of their own. She smiled wryly at the tongues of fire chasing each other from the clay and metal bases. No genie here to answer her wish — that aching wish — like the genies in the tales the camel drivers used to tell. In those days, this place was her father's *khan* and she was a girl certain that every dream would come true — noble husband, happy children around her. . .

Never mind — who had time for old longings tonight? There was so much to do, so many more people with the new census and heavy taxing. Their inn was the oldest and finest supper and sleep establishment in the area, but even if it weren't it still would have been crowded. Every inn was.

Making ready for the significant observance, Lydia and Jesse had hung the traditional lamb's tail with bitter herbs on the lintel and side posts of the door. But they also had hung Passover garlands of cedar on every crossbeam of the Great Room. A fresh scent was needed against the sweat of throngs! Tonight the greens made dancing shadows on the white-plastered walls in the crimson glow of the tall sconces. How many lamps Lydia had filled that day; every possible oval base and wall bowl had been topped over with fresh oil. And in between she had hauled endless jugs of water, assigned basins and linens, and given carpet rolls to guests who came ill prepared or who had met with misfortune along the way. She had listened to personal troubles and given advice; she had heard of new loves, scoffed at heroic tales; she had subdued the quarrels and bartering, too. Paying customers or not, Lydia would not have their inn turned into a marketplace.

All day she toiled, smiled, solved problems, and kept her ears open and her heart closed. Finally, when a sunset burnished with the dust stirred by hundreds of travelers had given way to the welcoming, flaming vessels on the tables, Lydia had ladled barley broth, and had served unleavened bread, fish, dates, figs, citrus from Canaan, and lamb roasted in terra cotta ovens beneath the shade of gnarled grey-green olive trees. Herod's armies could not have eaten more, nor have been more content.

All day Jesse saw to the animals as the travelers arrived. Camels, goats, sheep, dogs, and donkeys were secured at the stable beyond the inner court, near the cave that stored the new straw and the feed for the mangers. Nearby were Jesse's sturdy racks for reins and water skins. Now he closed up the inn for the night while Lydia put out the lamps.

One last lamp in the room. Just as the long-poled, silver-fan snuffer was to do its deed in Lydia's hand, she heard a knock. She listened for Jesse's weary shuffle toward the door and heard the iron bolt slide back as the mighty door opened, squeaking, straining, and scraping against the stone floor.

Muffled voices. Low pleading. Firm denials. Soft sobbing. Then wood scraping against stone. The bolt slid into place. Silence.

Lydia listened a moment. Then, "Jesse?"

No answer.

"Jesse?" Lydia flipped the long handle of the snuffer to the floor and tapped. "Jesse! What is it?"

No answer.

Using the snuffer handle as a cane, Lydia picked and tapped her way between tall wine jugs and broad breadbaskets, past benches still upturned on table tops in preparation for the floor to be swept and the bones to be gathered for the dogs. "Jesse. Jesse, answer me."

Entering the outer court, she rested on her pole and surveyed the scene. Jesse stood with his back against the bolted door, head bowed, chin on his chest, eyes closed, and his arms pressed behind him for balance.

"There was trouble?"

"No trouble."

"What then?"

"A young couple at the door . . ."

"So?"

"I told them we had no room."

"You've turned them away? What is wrong with you?"

No answer.

"Idiot! Foolish one! Seed of thistles! We can always make room!" She screamed. "Look at me! You actually turned people away?"

He did not raise his head but nodded assent slowly.

"Oie! We should be so rich!" She stood planted in the

stone, ready for war, feet apart, and both hands gripping the snuffer pole before her.

"Lydia, please. Don't start that. I did what I thought was best."

"May such wisdom fill the earth! May camels fly on the morrow and the morning sun rise in the west. May a brilliant new star blind the night sky."

"May you hold your peace!"

"Did you give them bread at least?"

"No."

"What? Not even bread?"

"I didn't want to delay their departure."

"Why?"

"I had my reasons."

"What reasons under the sign of Esther would restrain a morsel of bread at least! Bethlehem means house of bread; have you forgotten, Old Man? Does not our sign of the loaf swing now over the portal to this *khan*?"

"All that you say is true."

"What then? What explanation have you?"

"God forgive me, I did send them away empty but I was only thinking of you, Lydia."

Punctuating her anger, Lydia clicked the long snuffer's handle on the rough floor, up and down, up and down. "So, suddenly you are thinking of me! After a life's labor and a day's misery before a short night, you rob me by sending paying lodgers away and say you are thinking of me. May the pigs be so kind!"

"Lydia, Lydia . . ." He moved from the door with his arms and palms supplicating.

"Well, where have they gone? Who were they? Had they been here before?" Tap-tap-tap.

"Lydia, please. It should not be talked about. I told you — it was on your account that I did not extend welcome. Let it go."

"Jesse," she said, brandishing the snuffer like a Roman sword, "explain yourself or I'll wail before David's temple wall."

"All right," he said in resignation before his wife's fury. "Wail. Wail if you will. It is *because* of your wailing that I have sent them away. I will not soon forget the night six months ago when last you served as midwife—to the priest's wife, Elisabeth, remember? I came in from the stables to find you crumbled on that floor—there—clinging to the post, wailing! You would not be comforted, Lydia."

"God . . . had . . . given . . . *me* . . . no miracle!" She flung the words at him.

"You swore a vow never again to serve as a midwife."

Lydia's eyes flashed at him. "Don't mention that night, ever!"

"I know, I promised. I have kept my word until now. But you asked why I turned these young travelers away."

"So . . . may the reason be worthy of your strange behavior."

"Aah, Lydia." He shook his head, and his unwelcome tears glistened in the pale yellow light.

"Jesse!"

"All right. All right!" Then slowly he began," I turned them away because he is from the house of David." Jesse paused and toed the stone to avoid her stare. "She is cousin to Elisabeth."

The low hiss of waning lamps was the only sound. Long moments later Lydia asked, "You mean *that* Elisabeth . . . she who was well stricken in years and past the time of women whom I delivered?"

"The same."

"Oooh! Yaaah! Oie! Oie!"

The silver snuffer rattled on the threshold as Lydia dropped to her knees and rocked back and forth in agony. "Why Elisabeth? Why not a miracle for me? What have I done to deserve such reproach before men?"

"Peace, Woman. Peace from Jehovah."

"No! There is no peace from Jehovah, just as there is no child. It is my shame that the Lord has sealed my womb. I have not filled the measure of my creation! To be barren is to be dead and past feeling. It is my provocation, my anguish, my heartbreak that God does not love me. He had not remembered me as a handmaid!" She hid her face in the towel about her waist. "And now we have turned away kin of Elisabeth, descendants of David, and your own namesake. Is there no end to our sin?"

"There is more."

"More? What more can there be?"

"The young woman . . . she was heavy with child . . .
you are barren . . . I had to . . . I had to send them away . . .
because of you."

"Moses deliver me!" Back and forth she rocked and
groaned.

He knelt beside her then, and for the moment she allowed
his comfort, his soothing words. "It is of no matter now, Lydia.
It is over. We have lived long. We have crossed many dunes.
We have served others well. And . . ." he almost whispered,
"we loved each other once."

Suddenly Lydia stiffened, stifling her sobs. "And never
before have we turned anyone away! Go at once and find them,
Jesse. Go! They can't have gone far. Find them that we may be
redeemed and not be reason for God's wrath." She added a new
idea, "We'll make ready the stable."

Lydia scrambled to her feet and handed Jesse a lamp. It
flickered, sputtered, and recovered its orange-red flame as he
opened the door and went out.

Jesse found the tired couple still at the portals to the Inn of
Bethlehem. They were huddled on a saddle carpet against the
wall, the young father comforting the wife moaning in pain of
both heart and labor. As Jesse shuffled toward them, the rugged
young man began to apologize. They had traveled all the long
way from Nazareth that day. She had endured the donkey ride
over the rugged trail, which seemed to have hastened the delivery time. Neither of them knew much about these things, except
that she couldn't go on. They were sorry and anxious.

"Come!" Jesse beckoned them toward the inn, "My wife is
a midwife. She will know just what to do."

Jesse worried within himself as he volunteered Lydia's help.
Giving them space where the ripe woman could lay her head
was one thing, but to suggest that Lydia would supervise the delivery when she had vowed never to be midwife again was quite
another. If only Lydia wouldn't be so brittle and bitter.

"Come!" said Jesse, taking the donkey's leash. "We'll go
around to the stable. It's all we have left," he said, brightening,
"but it will be private from prying eyes and we'll make it

ready." One thing was sure: Lydia had supplies enough on hand for this kind of emergency.

Meanwhile, Lydia was making ready the stable. Murrey-paisley carpets had been hung over the corral rails to separate the animals from the fresh-hay bed where the couple would place their *kepeneks* for sleeping. She'd laid down clean goat pelts for extra comfort, and was pleased with her efforts.

When Lydia saw the frightened face of the lovely maiden, she realized that the girl was already in labor. She put aside her own vow in the urgency and efficiency that filled her experienced midwife's heart. She ran back to the inn and opened the store, gathering the new white wool felt to lay under the mother, a fresh sheepskin to put in the manger for the baby, and a virtual security blanket for it made from pure-wool fibers in natural brown, grey, beige, and white, and flecked with camel hair. She snatched up sea sponges, oil and ointment, yards of pure linen (no unkosher mix of fibers or *shatnes* in that household!) for swaddling clothes, and folds of softest Egyptian cotton for the countless changes required for a newborn. And there was the ball of narrow strips of lamb leather to tie off life dependancy between the infant and its mother. Last of all, she bound a fresh towel around herself before hurrying off to the stable.

She sent Jesse for jugs of wine, pitchers of cool water, and crocks of boiled water. Several basins were needed on hand to dip the baby in—first hot water, then cold—in case it didn't breathe right away.

But the baby did breathe. An inimitable cry broke the silence! Not even the animals had bleated until then, so controlled was all nature for that time. There was light enough, as well, for the heavens seemed blinded with light more luminous than the breaking dawn.

And so it was, that, while they were there, it was accomplished that the young mother was delivered of her firstborn son.

Lydia took the boy child, marveling anew at the incredible miracle of birth, of life, and of God's goodness. She washed the baby spotless from the process of birth. With each gentle stroke and long pat of the sponge, all the passions of her heart surfaced

—all the anguish and anger—and then were flushed away with her tears. Her eyes brimmed and spilled, brimmed and spilled, blending with the basin water and the anointing oil on the child's skin. She too, felt cleansed.

Lydia was an expert with newborns. Every newborn had about it an aura of heaven but this perfect babe radiated a quality of inner light that put her to weeping afresh as she worked. Joy engulfed her.

At last she wrapped the child in swaddling clothes and carefully laid him in his blushing mother's arms.

Streams of light filled the stable in the place where they were—prisms of blue, yellow, jade, lavender, amber, and vermilion.

The cattle and sheep stirred, lowing a kind of lullaby.

And there was peace.

Lydia hurried across the gravel of the inner court to the inn. There, Jesse waited, wondering and praying.

"It is a boy child! This one is right straight from heaven," she explained breathlessly, impulsively throwing her arms around him.

Jesse caught Lydia to him, smoothing her hair and tucking loose strands into the coral headband above her flushed cheeks.

"And you, Lydia?"

Lydia was thoughtful, subdued when she spoke, "It has been a remarkable experience of the Spirit . . . I felt . . . I felt . . . blessed." She burrowed her face into the folds of his robes. "Oh, Jesse!"

Swallowed in his embrace, Lydia, the innkeeper's wife, heard tender truth murmered in her ear. "My dear—my very dear—beloved of God as well as by me!"

2

Christmas . . .
The Shining
Season

Some say, that ever 'gainst that season comes
Wherein our Saviour's birth is celebrated,
The bird of dawning singeth all night long:
And then, they say, no spirit dare stir abroad;
The nights are wholesome; then no planets
  strike,
No fairy takes, nor witch hath power to charm,
So hallow'd and so gracious is the time.

— William Shakespeare (Hamlet)

2

Christmas . . . The Shining Season

Hallow'd, gracious! Ah! Christmas is a shining season. It is shining and glowing because the infant Jesus was born, because he lived, worked his miracles, and infused us with his spirit. It is a season that can be hallow'd and gracious if we follow the ultimate example Christ set in being gracious to others. He embodied peace, acceptance, patience, unselfishness, generous giving of self and spirit to others and to God the Father.

What shining possibilities might exist in our own celebration of Christmas when we try to be more like Jesus!

We suggest the following as steps toward that goal:

1. *Stretch the mind and heart toward a deeper understanding of Christmas*

What was the mission of Jesus? What of Mary, the mother of Jesus? What of Joseph, descendant of King David, protector of Mary, and guardian of the Christ child? What of God, the Father of Jesus who was his Only Begotten in the flesh? And what of Jesus—what of his sacred mission? Consider these lines:

Born in a stable,
Cradled in a manger,
In the world His hands had made
Born a stranger.

—Christina Rossetti

As we seek to understand and internalize the facets of the nativity trio and God the Father, the lifting and healing radiance of the season will fill our souls and make the day.

2. *Make the word of God part of the season*

Christmas can reach new heights for us through a study of the scriptures. Let us come to know the *full* story of Christmas by prayerfully studying the various records in which the details are found. Then we can accurately refer to the broader implications of the first Christmas. Then the season will become more meaningful to us. Read at least the complete Christmas account in Hebrews, Isaiah, 2 Nephi, Matthew, and Luke.

If you have trained in ballet you appreciate the prima ballerina's performance more fully than your neighbor who isn't so trained in this discipline. It's the same with art, athletics, science, and music. It is even more true with the discipline and knowledge of spiritual things.

We cannot find proper and satisfying solutions to our problems, or joy in relationships with others as well as with God, if we are not trained for success in that field!

3. *Plan as a way to improve the spirit of your Christmas*

Attitude and spirituality, gratitude and service are gifts of great value to those who share the celebration of Christmas with you. Start working on the spirit of your Christmas long before the season is in crisis! Everybody works together, then, to make the season a highlight of the year, a beacon for the year—a respite from stress and struggles, a renewal and refreshment, a guide for daily living. It will then be a time to gather up memories that simply cannot be matched for gladness.

4. *Find ways to help loved ones deepen their expectations of Christmas*

It takes psychology, I suppose, to deepen expectations in the appropriate way. Try presenting new options and loftier ideals for celebrating: Christmas in the intimate circle, Christmas in the extended circle, Christmas within, Christmas in the environment. For example, aren't the people wonderful who light up their houses, hang a bright star high on the chimney, or make Temple Square a marvelous symbol of beauty and light? Christmas in lights is a kind of winter gardening that in itself is a praise to God.

In the planning, learn to block the calendar a year ahead to remind of a new string of lights needed, the space of time it takes to accomplish certain traditional tasks. Also, block off time for personal fitness, the resting and grooming of body and soul necessary for full pleasure and sweet dispositions.

5. *Give Christmas its due*

If ever a political candidate would run on a ticket espousing Christmas Eve, as well as Christmas Day, as a legal holiday, that candidate would have my vote. Christmas Eve is the magic time. Anticipation stirs the air, surprises are under way, hope is comfort.

Such a magnificent occasion, such extensive preparation, such life-long memories and impact, deserves two full days. Yes, the English have Boxing Day but that is *after* the carols have ceased, the candles have melted, the tree has drooped, and the cousins have gone home. We are strongly suggesting that because of the glow Christ brings to the celebration, the whole day of Christmas Eve ought to be a legal holiday, a time for worship if you will. The absolute deadline for preparations should be the night before Christmas Eve. By that time package wrapping, fancy cooking, grocery and gift shopping, preparation of neighbors' gifts, house readying and personal grooming should long since have been completed. It makes a difference to dispositions and to opportunities to bring joy to others as well as readiness to enjoy the celebrations yourself.

Christmas is the Sunday of the whole year and it should be different from other times in our lives. At least, that's how I feel about it!

There should be a day to celebrate the sacred occasion—Christmas Eve—and a day to bask in the festivities of the season—Christmas Day. Carols are best until midnight Christmas Eve. By the time evening comes, peace, love, and graciousness abide in our hearts and homes, instead of frustration and hurt feelings brought on by poor planning, last-minute hassle. By the time Santa Claus has come and the gift opening gets under way, toys, games, and goodies seem to take precedence.

6. *Let peace begin with us*

There may not be peace on earth but there can be peacemakers. Blessed are the peacemakers of Christmas for they shall be called the season's shine-bringers.

Perhaps we shouldn't be surprised that there is no peace on earth. Prophets of every generation have warned against hard hearts and anti-Christ behavior. They have foretold the calamities that will increase as people become more sinful. The Lord himself said that "all men shall know that the day speedily cometh; the hour is not yet, but is nigh at hand, when peace shall be taken from the earth, and the devil shall have power over his own dominion. What I the Lord hath spoken, I have spoken, and I excuse not myself; and though the heavens and the earth pass away, my word shall not pass away, but shall all be fulfilled, whether by mine own voice or by the voice of my servants, it is the same." (D&C 1:35, 38.)

No matter how many days we celebrate, how oft we sing the carols of Christmas, how many gifts we give, peace for all the world will not arrive until the Prince of Peace comes again, and I suspect that he will not come until there is a people sanctified and prepared enough to receive him in peace and joy—regardless of what the rest of the world is up to.

We can insure peace in our own heart, in our own homes even if we seem powerless to bring peace to the world.

7. *Make Christmas the starting point of more Christlike behavior all year*

Christmas becomes a beautiful course in discipleship when what we have learned and felt we can effectively transmit to others all year.

You see, there are so many of our homes, affecting so many individuals, in which the spirit of contention is more prevalent than is the spirit of Christ — peace.

It is a heartbreak when people live as if Jesus had never been born, had never been placed in swaddling clothes, had never grown and waxed strong, had never changed the world forever for those willing to recognize and receive him.

Our task is to pattern our lives after the Savior, and then to help others come to know Christ so that they will have the desire to do the same.

Our task is to love others while they grow in this perfection. And we hope and pray that they will wait patiently while we struggle toward that end, too.

The way to make Christmas a forever shining thing is to be among those who bring the glad tidings of great joy, and to bring them appropriately.

A few years ago, I was making a just-before-Christmas pilgrimage to the Holy Land with a group of friends. Egypt was part of our itinerary, too — old Egypt, where Joseph took Mary and baby Jesus after the wise men told of Herod's plan to destroy all babies born at this time because one of them was the heralded future king.

Our group had been to Memphis one day. The trip on the touring bus had been long, hot, and tiring. On our way back to our accomodations, we stopped at a lonely roadside inn with the only restroom facilities for miles. Desperately primitive facilities they were, too!

Night had settled in. This was countryside without city lights. Except for the dim parking lights of the bus, only a faint cafe sign offered relief. The thick blackness about us was the more oppressive because we were in unfamiliar territory.

We seemed to be the only people about, until suddenly out of the darkness, appeared a person scraping along toward the bus on his bottom. As he positioned himself near the door of the bus we could see that he was a crippled beggar boy of ten or eleven. He had powered himself along with his arms, his useless legs stirring up enveloping clouds of dust. He was filthy.

It was shocking!

We supposed that he was the classic, heartbreaking example of child abuse that we had heard about among poor people in that area. His legs had been deliberately mangled in infancy, according to our guide, who knew because of that certain strange and ugly twist to them. This dreadful action was supposed to insure that his inevitable beggar's life would be more lucrative. We were heartsick at such circumstances.

The beggar was pitiful, of course. Surely more so because he was only a child and all alone, coming out of the darkness with his palms upturned in the universal gesture for a handout.

We had been strongly warned about not giving to beggars, but this situation seemed unique and compelling. We were fresh from Bethlehem, fresh from the land of the Good Samaritan. We were deep into the scriptures, so we weren't mere tourists but disciples of Christ. We loved children. These were reasons enough to quickly pass the hat for favored "American dollahs!" And we hadn't eaten the saltless sack lunches the tourist kitchen had prepared for us on the cruise ship. We could easily share those, too. We were in the fever of doing good.

I was standing at the door of the bus when the boy approached, asking for the proverbial alms. As the lunches and dollars were passed to me at the front, I reached them out of the door and into the arms of the beggar boy. As he collected them in his lap, he was amazed.

His face lit up before such bounty — until suddenly there was a rushing sound and out of the darkness came a band of beggars that literally piled upon the beggar boy. They fought him and each other for the gifts that we had given him. The driver of our bus slammed the door for our safety.

Suddenly, a man ran from the cafe and scooped the bleeding, bruised boy into his arms and disappeared. But the "Gadianton robbers" kept fighting over small stakes from a tourist bus.

It was a stunning experience.

We had learned the bitter lesson. Though our intentions were good, good intentions do not a Christmas nor a heaven make. Passing out gifts is neither a solution nor a substitute for the real intent of Christmas. We had the work of the babe of Bethlehem to do, the glad tidings and truth to spread, before such painful scenes as we had witnessed would be eliminated.

What if we, as a covenant people, did such a fine job of moving forth with the teachings and example of Christ that Christmas really existed all year long?

What if we lived in communities where fair trade was the rule; where people prospered from a harvest handled by eager labor; where there was no begging and no begrudging selfishness? And what if there were no tumult, contention, assault, incest, murder, rape, pornography, or even lying?

And what if people really listened to each other? What if yearnings were met, aching longings subdued, broken hearts healed? What if secrets were kept and gossip stifled? What if truth was treasured and lived by? What if people lifted up the hands that hang down and strengthened the feeble knees and carried each other's burdens in full purpose of comfort and solution? What if we could honestly, fully forgive *and* forget? What if the injured would love their enemies after the manner of the Savior on the cross?

What if no one suffered hurt feelings, self-pity, disbelief? What if husbands and wives learned to love each other best and children honored their parents? What if there were no child abuse, no sin at all?

What if all people prayed to a God they knew lived and in the certainty that he knew that they lived, too? And what if in God's name miracles were performed upon a believing public? The lame would walk and leap, the blind would see.

Though such a community actually has existed on earth is described in 4 Nephi of the Book of Mormon, how do we today make the peaceable walk? When we look to the time when the lamb and the lion shall lie down together without any ire, how do we help hasten the day?

I think that we can take at least three steps to move us steadfastly toward that perfect day. These are basic points, points which comprise the basis of all religious life. They deal with self, others, and God, fundamentals implicit in the first and great commandments of God.

Self: Study the scriptures to learn about Jesus, his life, his ideals, his hopes for mankind. In exactness we must follow Christ in spirit and laws, as did those Nephites of old. We grow in discipleship by first learning of him, and then following after him.

Others: We do unto others as the scriptures suggest. Be helpful instead of harmful to others. We should strive to be wise, not harming others in any way, even inadvertently as we hurt the beggar boy when our well-meaning efforts were ill-timed.

God: We should pray constantly to God until we feel close to him. Worship him. Obey him. Count our blessings from him. Love him. Let life be sweetened by following his will and his way.

Generally speaking, "his will and his way" are ways of love and peace. What his will is for us, in particular, can be made known to us through seeking guidance that comes through the Holy Spirit.

Here are some choice lines from some long-forgotten source that are poignant to me and seem to spell another dimension of being a believer and reaching for a true and shining Christmas:

> Blessed are they who understand my faltering step
> And my palsied hand.

> Blessed are they who know that my ears today
> Must strain to catch the things they say.

> Blessed are they who seem to know
> That my eyes are dim and my wits are slow.

> Blessed are they who look away
> When something is spilled at the table today.

> Blessed are they with a cheery smile
> Who will stop and chat for a little while.

> Blessed are they who never say
> "You've told that story twice today."

> Blessed are they who make it known
> That I'm loved and respected and not alone.

> Blessed are they who know that I'm at a loss
> To find the strength to carry my cross.

> Blessed are they who ease my days
> Of my journey home with their loving ways.

Karen Maxwell's family was getting ready for the shining season by assigning parts for the annual nativity production.

"What part would you like to play?" the kindly director asked one of the children.

"I want to be King Horrid!" the little fellow quickly replied.

And some people are "King Horrids" around Christmas. For them, somehow the shining season got lost in the shuffle of busywork and false notions.

Christmas can be a shining celebration if we seek the true meaning of the day, if we make the word of God part of the celebration, if we plan ahead, if we develop the right attitude, if we give Christmas its due, if we let peace begin with us, and if we strive to be more like Christ, whose life we celebrate this season.

Even if we are bereft of our favorite things, great or small, contemplation clarifies the secret of a shining season. It depends upon how high our vision is of Christ himself. How steadfastly we pursue a knowledge of Christ and a personal coversion to his ways will determine how shining our season—and our life —will be.

3

Suddenly
It's Christmas

The earth has grown old with its burden of care,
But at Christmas it always is young,
The heart of the jewel burns lustrous and fair,
And its soul full of music bursts forth on the air,
When the song of the angel is sung,

It is coming, Old Earth, it is coming to-night!
On the snowflakes that cover thy sod.
The heart of the jewel burns lustrous and fair,
And the voice of the Christ-child tells out with
delight
That mankind are the Children of God.

— Phillips Brooks

3

Suddenly It's Christmas

 It comes, Old Christmas, the day, the very moment that the big flakes finally fall in December.

It comes when you hear a certain piece of music of the
season that takes you back to another lovely time.

It comes, beloved holiday, on the wings of fragrance, with
the greeting from a cherished friend, in the wake of a kindness
given or received.

> Now comes Christmas,
> blazing with the pure radiance of joy,
> Now the air quivers with music,
> heard and unheard,
> and the remembered ringing of bells.
> Now is the time of giving and receiving,
> not things alone,
> but faith, hope and love,
> The darkness is past,
> and now the heart's sun rises.
> O may your life be filled with its light
> this Christmas day.

I read these theme-setting lines many years ago. We add another thought—Christmas comes when people behave toward each other in ways that make life less difficult. Small deeds are done spontaneously that meet a need, and suddenly it's Christmas, even if it is July.

My family's first Christmas in a new community offered the excuse to invite special neighbors to our home to celebrate the season. There was one young family who had won our hearts and we asked if they would provide the Christmas nativity since our own children and grandchildren were far away.

What a delight that evening was. We were almost strangers, and Christmas celebrations were supposed to be for families and dearest friends. But we soon felt that love for each other that night as the details of the birthday of Christ unfolded once more before us; it was a witness of the miracle of Christ's love.

The young father was in charge. He had arranged, rehearsed, costumed, and cajoled their five-year-old and three-year-old daughters into their roles of Joseph and Mary, respectively. Little Michael was a wise man. Brand-new baby Taylor —*too* new for a starring role—reminded us of the miracle of birth.

Lon also was narrator, so he had one eye on the scripture and the other on the "stage" entrance so that the actors could pick up the cue.

He began, "and Joseph also went up from Galilee, out of the city of Nazareth into Judaea, unto the city of David, which is called Bethlehem . . . to be taxed with Mary his espoused wife, being great with child."

In came Mary on the arm of Joseph. But what a surprise! That three-year-old Mary had stuffed herself in front to resemble her mother during her recent pregnancy.

We stifled our happy laughs in respect for the occasion and the seriousness with which the children were taking their parts. The performance continued with the leads getting to the proverbial inn and along out to the stable. There, Joseph cleaned and readied the manger while Mary rested.

Then the narrator continued, "And so it was, that, while they were there, the days were accomplished that she should be delivered. And she brought forth her firstborn son . . ."

At this point Mary suddenly jumped up and began a mighty shivering and shaking. She continued her wiggling until the stuffing that had fattened her tiny tummy dropped to the floor. Hidden in a pillow was a doll — a favorite doll, to be sure. Surprise! Her mother, Carrie, was most surprised of all.

Quickly the doll was snatched up from the floor by Joseph (whose name really was Jesika) and handed over to Mary (whose name really was Elizabeth). Mary anxiously took the baby (a doll whose name was *not* really Jesus) and wrapped and wrapped—no, wound — this baby in swaddling clothes (which really was Elizabeth's own security blanket for bedtime).

We all laughed and heartily applauded — and suddenly it was Christmas.

That little Christmas pageant took on a precious reality when those innocent children, who knew about new babies, all right, refused to skip the details.

We were so delighted with Mary's unique performance that the lively wise man (who really was twenty-month-old Michael) was nearly squeezed out of his opportunity to bring frankincense and myrrh to the new baby King. Michael's "myrrrrrh" sounded a lot like a kitten's purrrrr as he rolled the word off his tongue after much practice.

I thought back to a Christmas when our youngest was nine months old and his three-year-old sister played Mary. Mary placed that real live baby in her doll cradle-manger, and gave that baby Jesus such a rock that he rolled right over, cradle and all. I was horrified! He survived, but that presentation, too, was a pageant to stir Christmas into a new perspective. How gracious were Mary and Joseph to allow strange shepherds and foreign wise men to come close to their newborn! How patient they were all through the happenings of that sacred but trying time.

Elder Neal A. Maxwell once gave a talk about patience. It wasn't a Christmas message, per se, but something he included in his unique way seems especially applicable. "Inside our impatience there is sometimes, an ugly reality: we are plainly irritated and inconvenienced by the need to make allowances for the free agency of others. Patience is tied very closely to faith in our Heavenly Father. When we are unduly impatient, we are suggesting that we know what is best — better than does God."

Christmas stress and pressure can breed impatience but Christmas spirit can breed patience. Patience is a root of joy.

One church Christmas pageant comes to mind as an example.

Frankie was an especially handsome child. It was hard to disguise him as a shepherd, but he certainly didn't behave like an angel. He was, in fact, the kind of shepherd who wanted some creative input into the pageant itself. He was a kindergarten boy who was bursting with ideas about how the crowns ought to rest on the head of each little wise man. He fussed with Mary's robes and tucked under the swaddling clothes of baby Jesus before the program started.

Once the pageant was under way everyone in the cast was caught up in the beloved rendition of sacred events. Everyone except for Frankie, who was still fussing and fixing. He was a shepherd, and since he had never seen a walking stick with a crook on the end he was sure something was very wrong. So he straightened out the crook of aluminum foil at the end of his own staff. He performed the same service for his neighbor shepherd, who reached up and bent the foil back into a crook. Frankie reached over and straightened it out again. The bending and straightening became a bit of a scuffle. Finally the teacher became openly annoyed. She scolded Frankie severely enough to stir up the attention of the "little Mary." Mary then reached out her arm—the one that wasn't cradling baby Jesus—to touch Frankie and comfort him as she frowned at the teacher.

"You shouldn't be so angry," she whispered. "It's Christmas, you know!" She forgot that the microphone was clipped to her flowing mantle so the whole congregation got the wonderful message.

And how right she was. Though we all understood the teacher's motives very well, it was Christmas, and Christmas is about love. It was an unexpected bonus to the familiar Christmas story. That's what brings Christmas suddenly into being— unequivocal love.

There was a Christmas past that we now have labeled "The Orange Crate Christmas." At the time of that celebration, oranges were a delicacy and a delight, and they came wrapped individually in tissue and crated in a double-sided pine box.

People at a certain level of poverty, who also happened to be re-
sourceful, would obtain an orange crate from the grocer and use
it for a book case, a lamp table, or a storage chest, among other
things.

My husband had other ideas.

He was a sergeant in the army during this period of World
War II and was stationed at Bushnell Hospital in Brigham City.
On weekends he would commute from there to our little home
in Salt Lake City, Utah. The army pay was based on base living,
and four of us were trying to live off base as cheaply as one on
base.

We had no budget for Christmas and we had two toddlers
to play Santa for. So I sewed Raggedy Ann and Andy out of
trousseau linen — first things first! Our little son and daughter
would have at least one thing under the tree.

My husband had a surprise of his own. The area below the
house we were living in had been dug out just enough to allow a
stoker furnace to be installed as a gesture toward modern comfort. Jim spent long hours in that mole hole with two orange
crates.

I would call down to him often, "Jim, what is the attraction
down there?"

"Jim, bedtime long since! Can you come up for prayer?
(Air, too?)"

"Jim, what *are* you doing down there?" Even if Jim hadn't
declared it out of bounds until Christmas, I wouldn't have
wanted to go down there. But I kept contact.

"Jim? Is everything okay?"

He was planning his own surprise and I felt like a stander-
by when a child has fallen in an abandoned well. If there is some
response from below, people are heartened and the digging goes
better.

So I held the household together on the basis of muffled
grunts from the dungeon and carols from the radio.

Christmas Eve came and the toddlers, one and two, were in
bed. Jim went down once more to the cellar and emerged Santa
Clause incarnate! He brought forth orange crate chairs for the
children. The crate's dividing piece now formed each chair's sitting spot. Once Jim had removed the top and two sides of one

end, there was a back rest. To provide the support, two-by-four hunks had been nailed into place. To provide stability to the base, similar hunks had been attached. We are talking hunks!

A deafening clunk resounded when he lifted each chair through the opening connecting Santa's workshop in our basement with the kitchen linoleum. I had some idea of how heavy these kinder chairs really were because of that clunk as well as the grunts Jim made when he hoisted them up.

I was terrified the children would be maimed for life if these chairs tipped over on top of them. But the chairs went under the tree and added a Christmas touch with their bright paint.

However, the chairs never did become standard play equipment in the nursery. The size was right but the heft was wrong.

"They'll grow into them," Daddy explained. "We'll bring them upstairs again when the kids are bigger."

"They'll never be big enough for those chairs," I thought, but kept silent thinking of the pride in his eyes when he first showed them to me. It was the sight of a love I'll long remember.

Something else happened on that Orange Crate Christmas that underscores the goodness of people. A postal delivery man knocked at our door mid-morning Christmas Day. I was impressed that he had given up his own Christmas morning to complete deliveries, making certain that others weren't disappointed.

He handed us a large surprise package from Betty Waugh Sellman who was living in California. We had had little contact for several years. I was a teenager when this woman, an editor, changed my life by giving me my start with the *Tribune-Telegram* as a daily society columnist. I came to love her, working under her guidance, but never more than at this moment when this box appeared.

We all helped with the opening.

Inside was the most welcome gift: Layers of clothing her own child had either outgrown or rarely used. However, everything was exquisitely cleaned, ironed, folded, and tissued. The quality and high fashion of the undershirts, the socks, the shoes, the coats, the hats, the dresses, and the shirts proved to be something our own children could never have had. We were overcome.

Hand-me-downs, some might call such a gift, but it was Christmas for us and we decorated the orange-crate chairs with the items. Our toddlers had a satisfying time rearranging the clothing pieces and putting socks on the stuffed hands of the dolls.

Several short incidents have underscored the idea that one feels the spirit of Christmas when someone does something for you or for someone else, after the manner of Jesus.

I was a passenger in a car riding along a dangerously busy street in a large city where traffic in town was one big headache. The driver of the car, Kiki Knickerbocker, was an unusually chic and vibrant young mother. She also was serving as president of the stake Young Women. As she pulled behind several cars stopped for a red light, a street vender waved a bottle of windshield cleaning solution and a roll of paper towels.

No one in the line of cars ahead had accepted his deal. As he approached her car — only seconds before the light changed and before she would have to move forward on her way — she rolled down her window and said, "Do what you can!"

How that man hustled to clean her windshield, even risking the traffic pattern to reach the passenger side of the windshield. She handed him a dollar and he called, "God bless you!"

"He already has!" she called back.

And for me — and, I think, for the window washer — suddenly, it was Christmas. My heart warmed with hope for the next generation when she explained, "I know we are not supposed to encourage that sort of thing, but I see so many beggars in this city and when somebody is willing to work, I think they deserve all the help we can give them."

She is a woman as lovely inside as out. Would it were true of all of us in these days of cosmetic surgery, coloring, make-up, fashion, and figure toning.

On another occasion I was a guest in a home where workmen had finally showed up to start a long-awaited project. It was not good timing for the hostess with guests in the house. The before-school minutes with the children were interrupted by the demands of the workmen who needed to get going for the day. In the confusion, the thoughtful sister suddenly noted that her thirteen-year-old brother had walked to the pick-up point for the school bus and had left his lunch on the kitchen counter. The girl was busy with her own school preparations, but without a moment's consideration — and with certainly no word from her unaware mother — she announced the problem and took action.

"Jake's forgotten his lunch! Wow!"

Meaning that teenager will starve to death! She grabbed the bag and took off across the lawn, scaled a corral fence, sprinted down the street and out of sight. She came back with the sack: the bus and the boy had left.

Her explanation to her mother about the situation was, "Mother, I told you I had to train more to beat the school running record! I was too slow to help Jake."

Suddenly it was Christmas — a warm-heart time, do-unto-others time, don't-have-to-be-commanded-in-all-things moment.

In Miami, the LDS meetinghouse has a row of garbage cans with heavy-hinged lids that are buried in the concrete outside the rear entrance to the building, close to the kitchen area. We came out of the Sunday meeting to find a momentary crisis. A preschool age child pushed past us toward his father, clearly a financial struggler if appearances were any indication.

"Daddy, Daddy! Help!"

Father and son hurried to the row of garbage cans. Children were animatedly considering the situation. Father was scolding — Sunday shoes were unheard of in that family, and that boy had lost a shoe — from his *only pair of shoes.*

The father was angry, full of advice and threats. The little shoeless child was bereft and in tears. And then a wonderful thing happened. A ten-year-old in his Sunday clothes — white long-sleeved shirt, clip tie, and sharply creased cream-colored slacks, dropped to his stomach on the dirty surface surrounding the garbage units and helped. Someone held up the heavy lid and the "saving friend" slid up his shirt sleeve before digging into the garbage where a big bully had buried the shoe.

"Daddy, Daddy! He got it! He got it!" cried the victim.

We all clapped and praised the young helper.

"Oh, I like to do good deeds," he said, buttoning his shirt sleeve, and puffing up just a bit.

Absolutely, this is a royal generation climbing life's ladder. Suddenly it was like Christmas, such joy there was inside of me.

I watched a bigger boy get down on all fours like a horse, offer his hand as a stirrup, and help a toddler stand up on his back next to a high drinking fountain. That was some thirsty child and one clever, patient friend kneeling there. He didn't have to do that, you see. On his level, it was a great deed. Friends were waiting. Mother might even have some critical observation about knees and pant legs. A certain discomfort and awkwardness accompanied the procedure. But he did it, and nobody told him to.

Suddenly I wanted to raise the roof with the Hallelujah Chorus!

When Bea Taggart showed up at our door with the peaches from our laden trees, picked and bottled for our family while I convalesced from serious surgery, I could have wept. It was only September, but Christmas came early that year.

Christmas came late the year our first son returned from his mission. Everyone in the family from the oldest down to the youngest and least disciplined had agreed to postpone the family celebration until beloved big brother returned from duty to God in Europe. The first thing we did was to kneel in family prayer, and during those moments I heard our missionary trying to supress sobs. I knew he was glad to be home but . . . then, it struck me.

He was homesick for the good Saints he'd worked with in Germany. He had left loved ones to come back to strangers, strangers to whom he was related, but who had grown up and changed while he was away. And in a different house, at that.

Suddenly it was Christmas for me. You see, I knew then that the mission had taken within his heart. It was witnessed to me that he had known Jesus and done his work. I could see, hear, and feel the fruits of such love. The reaction wouldn't have been so deep otherwise, because this young man was a family man.

There just may be no more important effort we could make than putting the ideal of Christmas into our lives. It proves a blessing beyond belief to learn what the dear Christ child represented. When we apply his example and his principles to our relationships and opportunities, then finally life will be less difficult for us all. Someday, as the good tidings spread sufficiently by a corps of prepared disciples, perhaps we will know peace among people and heaven on earth.

The right kind of Christmas celebrating can hasten the day. People learn better the vital lessons of joy when their hearts mellow with memories and their beings fill with the delights of this sacred holiday.

Even though David Grayson's writings are collected by a limited group, he is a gentle, wise, and practical armchair philosopher whose ideas are well loved. He wrote something about Christmas that sums my feelings:

"I sometimes think we expect too much of Christmas Day. We try to crowd into it the long arrears of kindliness and humanity of the whole year. As for me, I like to take my Christmas a little at a time, all through the year. And thus I drift along into the holidays—let them overtake me unexpectedly—waking up some fine morning and suddenly saying to myself: 'Why, this is Christmas Day!' "

And that is one great worth of the season . . . to become stirred up into generous giving of heart, mind, time, and goods until Christmas demeanor, Christmas feeling—Christlikeness —is our way of life always.

4

Christmas—
Joyful and
Triumphant

O come, all ye faithful,
Joyful and triumphant;
O come ye, O come ye
To Bethlehem.

4

Christmas—Joyful
and Triumphant

e all remember the tune, but it is more challenging to remember the significance of this beloved Christmas carol's opening lines: "O come all ye faithful, joyful and triumphant." These words may well represent the most exact meaning of Christmas. Faithful people, believing in Christ and trying to follow his ways, are joyful because they are triumphant over the small annoyances, the pesky impositions, and the more demanding trials of life. If this thought crossed our minds as many times as we've sung the words of the old carol, we'd be well on our way as disciples of the Lord Jesus.

Countless stories tell of the goodness of people. Most communities have their kindly souls and thoughtful neighbors as well as their share of real heroes. At Christmas people often rise to great heights in giving and in showing love. We may even surprise ourselves. But being joyful and triumphant, at Christmas (at least!) can also mean striving for peaceful relationships laced with unselfish surprises. It is honoring our precious ties in a special way.

Many people diligently, if not always joyfully at first, persist in celebrating Christmas because they have a subconscious craving for their own roots. A person develops a strong sense of personal identity when he maintains connections with his past, psychiatrists have explained. Christmas offers an excuse to do just that. It is the hearts of the children turning to the fathers, and vice—versa, that we learned about in genealogy class!

To reach out in joy, to triumph over all that might separate us from our roots, is to feel a link with the Christ child. This reaching can season our celebration with a certain sweetness and can lay a pattern for better times for the years ahead. Be that as it may, Christmas as we know it today is one of the big success stories in the history of mankind.

A Florida Jewish synagogue was vandalized by young ruffians who wrote obscenities in spray paint and hung posters featuring the swastika and a greeting from so-called Christians demanding "Die Jew!" They left the place with shabby remnants of Christmas garlands dragged through all manner of filth and garbage.

Religious leaders from neighboring churches came at once to offer support. The senior class of the high school marched in like an army to clean the place up.

On a recent trip I visited a lovely home where the father was a new member of the church. He had come from an environment in which the lifestyle was gracious and exclusive. He was amazed to learn of the goodness, unselfishness, and caring of others in his new church. He was making great strides in conforming his life to the Savior's example.

As I was getting ready to leave, Brad came into my room with their nine-year-old daughter and they brought a bundle of gifts. These were delightful items, useful and valuable even though they bore the label of the company he worked for, and had been used as give-away items in a promotional event.

After the giving, I started to thank him and he said, "Oh no! This is Abby's idea. These gifts are from her. She asked me to bring something to you. Thank Abby. Thank Abby. Don't thank me."

I mentioned that I liked gifts best where together people help other people—like a dad helping his daughter—bring joy to someone else. Cooperative giving spreads the blessings. For example, a family who holds council at Christmas, or well before, will be blessed with a fullness of spirit when they raise important questions: "With whom can we share our surplus?" "Who needs our help today?" "What can we sacrifice to make someone else happy?" "What can we do to make our gifts more pleasing?"

A Cambodian refugee family moved into our son's beautiful home. They were treated with respect and allowed to function as they chose in the brand-new bathroom and bedrooms assigned to them. They chose to cook in the shower stall, wash clothing in the toilets, and sleep on the floor. They sat in a circle on the queen-size bed to eat. Except on rare occasions, they chose to eat together, away from our son's large family.

As the weeks passed, the refugees learned many new skills and became comfortable mingling with strange people. They had had to adjust from life in a refugee camp which, for four years, had been narrow—an eight-foot square plot had been marked off in the compound dust as their "home." They had been farmers, used to open fields and personal freedom. Confinement, near starvation, illness, deprivation of any small conveniences or helps for living added to their suffering and humiliation.

Jamie's family did everything possible to help these good people move forward in their new life—everything including leaving them alone when they needed to be left alone: sometimes do-gooders can smother recipients with their well-meaningness!

When at last the visitors' own new home had been arranged and they were ready to be on their own, our large extended family held a gala shower for the immigrants! It was a glorious outcropping of the Christmas spirit, a remembrance of our own pioneer ancestry who crossed the plains for freedom's sake. And the gifts were generous and varied, practical and beauty-bringing, ranging from a vacuum cleaner to a potted pear tree.

Christmas, however, came *after* the gifts were opened!

An exchange of love and respect took place, a sharing of gratitude for the kindness extended. The refugee family and the host family members had learned valuable lessons from each other. Tributes were shared via an interpreter, though no translator was needed to define affection and gratitude. It was wonderful! Our extended family extended even further that night, and the non-Christian newcomers to our circle were grateful most of all for such a wide circle of loving brothers and sisters "in front of the great God."

Although the party was for them, the blessing turned out to be for us.

We are talking about the highest kind of living, the most joy-bringing kind of celebrating, the most glorious gift we can return to God.

A neighbor hired a youth to do Christmas gift deliveries for his company. When the assignment was finished, the business-man handed the young teenager a festive Christmas card in which was tucked a crisp, bank-new fifty-dollar bill for his work. My neighbor could have written a check or could have handed over a crumpled collection of bills. But the man put forth extra effort to bring delight to the youth who had never seen a fifty-dollar bill before!

Scott was eleven when he got a paper route. He had only one goal in mind: he loved his mother and wanted to buy her a really fine Christmas gift, and he wanted the independence of having his own money to do it with. So he delivered papers, collected the money, and stored the savings away in a quart-size canning jar, a jar over which he had glued pictures cut out from magazines so that the contents of the jar would be private. He hid the jar deep in the clothing of his dresser drawer.

As the weeks and months passed, the little savings grew. Every so often, Scott would have to squish down the bills in order to fit more money in the jar. Finally, Christmas was close enough that he felt he could take the money down to Auer-bach's Department Store and buy a gift.

He had been looking at necklaces, dresses, purses, vases, books, dishes, and perfume. He hadn't decided what he wanted until one day he saw a handsome necklace designed after the one that Elizabeth Taylor wore in the movie *Cleopatra*. They had a picture of Elizabeth as Cleopatra on display to promote the necklace. Scott thought that it was the prettiest necklace he'd ever seen on the world's most beautiful lady — except for his mother, of course. He was loyal to his mother. She could do justice to such an elaborate spray of stones on the Egyptianstyled collar necklace. But the gift would cost more than he had. He'd wait. He asked the clerk if she could save the necklace for him until future collections were gathered from the paper route. They made the arrangements and she took some of his money as a down payment.

Scott was excited. The more he thought about the necklace the surer he became that he wanted it for his mother. He thought about how she had made his costume for the school play and had stayed up late nights to do it. He thought about the time he had injured his leg and she drove him back and forth, between home and school, never grumbling. She had sat by his hospital bed and read wonderful stories to him, too. Mother could read aloud and recite the scriptures by heart with great expression. Oh, Mother was special!

Scott talked to the owner of a neighborhood bakery who then let Scott come in before school in the morning and help him by lifting heavy bags of flour for the day's baking. Those were cold mornings and bed seemed especially inviting, especially when his brothers were still sleeping. But then Scott would go in to kiss his mother good-bye and learn that she had already packed him a lunch for the day. She was worth this effort, and how surprised she would be to get this wonderful necklace, just like a movie star's — *a movie star and a queen!*

Shortly before Christmas, mother was suddenly taken to the hospital for serious surgery. There was a growth in the front of her neck and the doctor made an incision at the base of her throat from under one ear across to the other. The family was frightened. They fasted together and had prayers morning and night. Daddy called the temple and asked them to put her name on the special prayer roll. Everybody helped around the house to try and take Mother's place. The school lunches were dry and laundry piled up, but the neighbors brought in good dinners so the family managed to get along all right. But with Christmas coming and Mother sick, nothing seemed right.

Scott had kept his secret of the necklace to himself for many weeks but now thought he should get it from the store and give it to Mother right away — just in case she didn't get home for Christmas. To know how much her son loved her might help her feel better.

Scott's dad got permission from the doctor and the hospital staff to take Scott to Mother's hospital room. With his present in hand, his heart pounded with excitement. What a surprise!

He hurried into the elevator and then down the long hall with his dad struggling to keep up with him. How happy Mother would be!

No matter how many times Dad had asked Scott what the gift was, the boy wouldn't tell. This was his very own gift to Mother. And now the time had come to present it to her. Christmas Day itself couldn't be any better than this.

Scott hadn't seen Mother for two weeks. She had been too ill for children to come in. He was shocked at how thin and fragile she appeared. Her neck was bandaged and she could hardly turn her head.

But Dad told Scott that he could give her a kiss on the forehead. The boy then placed the package on top of his mother's hands folded across her waist. Daddy explained quickly that Mother's tears were because she was so happy to see him: she agreed with a small nod of her head. Scott stood at the foot of the bed where they could see each other while she opened the gift. He was afraid to help her, to touch her. She seemed like a stranger to him. He was afraid he might hurt her, too. So Daddy helped her.

Off came the beautiful wrappings of silver and blue that the clerk at Auerbach's had put on the box for him. Then the lid of the box came off—silver with pressed designs all over. Then Dad lifted the soft flat cotton square in the shape of the box. And there, for Mother to see, was the spray of silver, turquoise, and coral with long, gold teardrops evenly forming a Cleopatra collar.

Dad took the heavy necklace from its box and held it up for Mother to see. She gasped, "Scott! Where? . . . How much? . . . What did you do? . . . Oh, Scott!"

"I love you, Mother. I started to buy it before you got sick. You have to get better now, don't you see? I've been paying for it for three months! You just have to get better, don't you see?" Scott was crying now, too. Even Dad had to blow his nose.

"Oh, Scott, my darling," said Mother.

"Now you can't wear it! All those bandages," Scott suddenly realized.

"Ah, but I can hold it close to me all day and night until I *can* wear it!" explained Mother. And she did. Dad found a hospital blanket pin and, attaching it to the necklace, pinned it to Mother's gown. "One day very soon — maybe for Christmas, or maybe for my January birthday — I'll be able to wear it. I'll come home, Scott. Anybody who would buy me a gift like this deserves one more good lunch in his life, at least. I'm the mother who will fix it, too."

I remember sitting in the congregation of a particular Christmas program in our ward. The young woman speaking was lovely to behold. Her eyes sparkled; her cheeks gently flushed with the emotion of her talk. She actually radiated a warming glow as she stood at the pulpit with her chin slightly lifted, telling about the purpose in the birth of Jesus.

"How her Heavenly Father loves her!" my neighbor whispered.

"How do you know!" I questioned.

"Why, for any number of obvious reasons," came the firm reply. "Look at her!"

We continued this intriguing discussion as we left the chapel, a discussion that soon turned into a blessing-counting session of our own. God loved us, too — beginning with our own blessings because of the birth of Jesus and all that that meant. We all enjoy great and good gifts from God. In addition, there are numerous subtle ways that he has graced all of us.

Families do things their own way on Christmas Day, and mostly that's how people want it to be, until somebody leaves home to marry — joining his or her roots with somebody else's.

Our family was an all-out family for Christmas, going for the full treatment within what budget and energy would allow. When we got in gear for the season, we were busy with much preparation in getting, giving, eating, decorating, and doing good deeds; we filled the house with good fragrance, good music, good art, and some well-loved but not-so-marvelous renderings from the elementary school days.

Other people do it other ways. You do it yours. And that is

how it should be, of course. It's absolutely fine, in fact — unless one of the simple celebrators marries one of the all-out-for-the-whole-show people.

And that is exactly what happened in our family.

These two had been married for a few delightful months when Christmas neared, and our daughter asked her new husband when they could go and get their Christmas tree. He said they weren't going to get a tree. He came from a family of long-standing conservationists and they didn't believe in destroying a forest for a pagan custom.

So much for Christmas as she had always known it. So much for "personal identity" for either of them if the argument ensued.

The day she called for a formal appointment with me I knew that trouble existed in the new nest. She talked of loving, wondering how she could love this man so much when they didn't agree on something as basic as a Christmas tree! I listened for a time and all the while wondered if we had done her a favor, after all, by making such a big celebration of Christmas.

When it was my turn to talk, I expressed my gratitude to her that she had loved growing up in our home, with our kind of celebration for the season of joy which marks the most important event in history. Then, I expressed gratitude for the very fine young man she had brought into our family. I was certain his good parents felt the same way about our "jewel." Clearly, this young man felt strongly about his own upbringing, his own family's understated celebration and traditions.

Background. Stalemate. Hard questions.

Could celebrations so different ever be reconciled! Could remembrances of how Christmas always had been be put aside for someone else's memories? Whose roots mattered most? Which celebration was better, more appropriate? Who was right?

I responded quickly to the last question, "Who is right?" to suggest my personal philosophy in these tight squeezes marriage presents to us: "Would you rather be right or loved?"

Finally, we talked about the right of each family to establish its own traditions. Family life was about compromise.

When children enter into family life and grow up they bring even more change into traditions that a couple has established. Unless people cooperate, unhappiness, argument, and even estrangement result.

Then we talked about traditions and symbols. Nothing sacred existed about how many verses were sung, of which carol, or how the turkey was stuffed. Whether the cranberries were sieved or served whole, plain or with grated orange, and whether the dressing was moist or dry crumbs, mattered little as well. Christmas really didn't depend on whether there was a tree. What it did depend upon was an abiding love in *their* home and happiness in what *they* were building. The day that those two were married, a new family began — an eternal, forever family was their goal. *That* family was not obligated to do things in exactly the way either of their parents had done. They were neither bound to celebrate sensibly if sparsely, nor foolishly and elaborately nor somewhere in between. They could prayerfully and carefully talk things over (a procedure of marriage that needs another book to explain!), eventually deciding what counted for the two of them as they began the traditions of their family Christmases.

Well, they did that. It turned out that they had a tree, but one that came in a pot so that it could be planted in the garden in the spring!

Christlikeness brings more joy to the season of Christmas than pursuing one's personal identity. I may be at odds with the psychiatrists about that idea, but it seems that ideally the next step after a potted tree, or of some other symbol of the season, may well be that one partner will say to the other, "I love you more than a tree or a tradition. Let's do what will make *you* happy!"

And that is how I learned to like roast beef with rice instead of mashed potatoes and gravy! You win some and you lose some, but what is gained in the compromise is of more value.

Trees or not, simple or strenuous celebrations notwithstanding, home is the place we want to be for Christmas. Like homing pigeons, we want to return, either in person or in spirit, to where we were loved anyway and to where familiar things once meant security, and to where everything would be all right because either Dad could fix it or Mom would kiss it better.

Christmas can be a training ground for the rest of the year. I had a young man pour out his heart (grievance!) about the fact that he didn't want his wife changing the living room furniture around while he was at work and without his permission or agreement. It was painful. He felt strongly. So did she. And if furniture matters more than delighting one's spouse, peace in the home, love in hearts, and a firm, lasting marriage, it is easy to predict a sour outcome.

Christmas is about loving more than having one's own way. Jesus, at his moment of crisis, cried out to the Father and suggested that perhaps "the cup" could pass, that he might not have to go through the terrible suffering of atonement, crucifixion. But then he said, "Thy will, not mine." He yielded his heart. And that made all the difference. Such incredible unselfishness makes us stand all amazed!

When Christmas celebrating helps us become more Christlike, we have won the worth of the season.

Joyful and triumphant!

Let's take another angle to this. What about love given that is not returned? Rejection? Abandonment? Heartbreak? Ingratitude? Casting away precious overtures? Why, some might ask, be the one who gives in all the time, who apologizes, who is the peacemaker, who is unselfish, who loves "anyway"? Why be the rug to someone else's careless, even selfish, footsteps?

What of wasted effort, wasted affection, unrequited love?

If a person is in a situation that seems heartbreaking as Christmas nears, what brings forth healing so that the season can go forth happily for him or her?

During such a time in my own life, I was on an assignment that took me to Cambridge, Massachusetts, several different times over a period of months.

Henry Wadsworth Longfellow's home was on a street that I walked for renewal each time I was in that area. It is a classic two-story home attractively painted: creamy butter with white trim. I'd look at that tasteful and solid "homey" house and reflect upon the man's wisdom and his example. During this time I learned some lines of his that express what I feel about unrequited anything, including affection at Christmastime. These lines have to do with affection but can be read in terms of

Christmas preparing, Christmas sacrifices, Christmas giving,
Christmas patience:

Talk not of wasted affection, affection never was wasted,
If it enrich not the heart of another, its waters, returning
Back to their springs, like the rain, shall fill them
    full of refreshment;
That which the fount sends forth returns again to the fountain.

This is Christmas at its peak, really. It is about being joyful
and triumphant because the right things are done for the right
reasons, no matter what anybody else chooses to do or be. In
other words, no one can truly spoil your Christmas. You simply
don't allow it. You have more faith than that in the institution
of the celebration itself, as well as in God and in yourself. To go
forth and give and serve, regardless of gratitude or affection or
understanding reciprocated or not, is to be joyful and triumphant in this most exquisite of established opportunities.

We have recently learned this lesson in our family.

Under very difficult circumstances, we did extensive
remodeling on a house. The building contractor with whom we
worked was an answer to prayer. That is not a trite phrase, but
a statement of fact. We prayed, and he came. The fruits of his
labor proved it so.

Mr. J. rose to the occasion of our circumstances and gave
more of himself than the bid would financially support. He
loved the house. He took pride in his work. He delighted in the
problems he helped solve and in the beauty he had a part in pro-
viding. He worked on our home as if it were his own. But it
wasn't: one day the project was finished, and he turned and
walked away.

Creative output requires enormous investment of self and
incredible unselfishness, too. An author writes a book through
prayer, study, energy, financial investment, and hard work.
The project is finished and sent forth—turned away from. The
artist is the same. Parents produce children, love and care and
mold them. The children leave the home, and leave behind
parents and childhood as well. What of these creators? Was it
worth the effort?

In planning celebrations for this glorious holiday in honor of the Savior—our light and example of loving—we face the possibility of investing tremendous physical, financial, and emotional resources that could well be lost in the cluttered shuffle of other people's lives and schedules, other modifications and memories. Is the sacrifice worth it?

Is Christmas going to be ruined because somebody didn't express gratitude in word or deed; because the gorgeous trappings were overlooked; because somebody came late, or left early, or didn't come, or didn't care, because feelings were hurt over whether Luke was read by firelight or not; because permission wasn't asked or a discussion wasn't held over every aspect of the arranging, the decorating, the gifting, the guest list, the programming, the spending, or whatever, whatever, whatever?

God grant that we can rise above anger, self-justification—above putting the things that matter least before the things that matter most. God grant that for this season, at least, we can be joyful and triumphant over self as well as over circumstance.

An experience in an Idaho parking lot may lend valuable perspective here. A car pulled into the slot against a variety-store entrance. The back seat was piled high with packages and signs of celebration decorations. The driver was a young married woman, and her father sat in the passenger seat. He was obviously distraught and disoriented. She turned to talk to him before getting out of the car. He pushed her away from him, and before she could get the door locked on his side, he opened the door and was out into the lot hurrying away from her.

He was probably a victim of Alzheimer's disease and had lapsed into one of the angry outbursts that are a sad part of the problem. By the time she could get to him, dodging traffic and praying that he would be able to dodge the cars as well, he was in an uncontrolled rage. She tried pulling him back to the car; but he wouldn't be led or coaxed, and she was afraid he'd get lost or hurt. The more she approached him, the more he lashed out at her with his arms, legs, and abusive language. She argued and shouted back. She tried to reason with him. She pleaded with him, desperate and embarrassed. She tried pulling him along toward the car. People all wanted to help but no one really could. He was totally out of control. Several times she turned and walked away. And then in his frantic actions, he lost his balance and fell to the ground, crying like a baby. The daughter stood over him for a moment, studying him. He had been the strength of her life for so many years, and now his utter helplessness broke her heart. She knelt down to him and cried also. "Oh Dad! My Daddy! My dear Daddy." At last she could wrap her arms around his neck and put her cheek against his, tears dissolving into tears, cheek to cheek.

And the miracle occurred. The old man melted. Her frantic, audible prayers, uttered as she chased him about the parking lot, had been answered! Her loving, comforting, Christlike manner soothed the man whom she no longer knew or understood.

In a few moments she helped him up with the aid of a stranger, and got him back into the car, kissing him repeatedly as she buckled him in his seat belt. Thinking better about going into the store, I suppose, she climbed into the car beside her father and, joyful and triumphant, drove off.

The late Wayne Brown, distinguished financier, was giving a Christmas message in church. His theme was the importance of putting self last for a season, at least. And then, if a season could be stretched into a year, a lifetime of peace on earth—or at least in that person's heart—might be a possibility.

He used a recollection from childhood to prove a point. His mother sent him across town to collect some overdue rent. She had reminded the tenants several times that her family needed the rent that was due to them.

The boy didn't get the rent. The people said they simply didn't have the money. All the way home he thought of what he could do, what he could say, to pacify his mother. Times were hard. He knew how much his family needed the money. His mother was a widow without any other support for her growing family.

"Mother, I couldn't collect the rent," he finally reported. "We don't need Christmas as much as those people need our rent money."

"Son, you are absolutely right. You march right back down there with this loaf of bread and this tub of honey. Be sure you leave a blessing on the house as well."

"Mother, I'm only ten years old. I can't say stuff like 'God bless you!' "

"Yes, you can. And you will. Practice with me right now and then you'll see how easy it is to comfort others."

The businessman telling the story laughingly added, "Mother was a poor businesswoman, but she was one wonderful Christian lady. And I have to admit that I felt pretty good myself, as I ran all the way back to our renters with bread instead of recriminations."

Joyful and triumphant . . . with good deeds at Christmas.

5

Christmas— Roots of Joy

Joy to the world, the Lord is come;
Let earth receive her King!
Let ev'ry heart prepare him room,
And heav'n and nature sing, . . .

— Isaac Watts

5

Christmas—Roots of Joy

What are the roots of your joy? What traditions are most important at Christmas? Have you assessed what prompts the spirit of Christmas to touch you or, on the other hand, what destroys the feeling of the season?

Give yourself a gift by analyzing what the roots of your joy are, and then cultivating them. Things could be even better one day!

Values about Christmas change with experience, circumstances, age, and health. Take this into consideration when you begin to dig into the roots of your joy. To some it matters greatly how people deck their halls, whether Christmas cards are printed and enclosed in foil-lined envelopes, or whether greetings are hand signed and boast a personal note. Some view the mass Christmas-card mailings as a needless nuisance and ignore them, instead going forth with elaborate gifts for the neighbors. Some want all the troops in for the celebrating. Others want the day nice, slow, quiet, and geared to time for reading the new book from Santa. Some insist on hitting all the Christmas concerts: The *Nutcracker*, the Dickens Christmas Festival. Some want the family to dress up for the day. Others spend it in robe and new 'jamas with all meals for the full day hot off the buffet bar laden with gourmet snacks and Christmas goodies.

To some celebrators, Christmas isn't Christmas without two trees — one for the children and one for show. Some have special dinnerware designed with yuletide motifs. Some line up their antique Santas or pose their antique dolls among the centerpiece greens. Some quilt everything. Others are strictly silver-and-shine people with door decor, mantel and gift carrying forth the theme.

A family or neighborhood progressive Christmas dinner would be eye opening as to what people enjoy as the only way to get ready for the holidays.

To some, Christmas has little to do with hanging holly or lighting candles, wrapping presents or baking shortbread. It has everything to do with raising the joy level for those around them. Christmas exists wherever joy exists, and without personal trappings — it needs only warm hearts, gentle people, and a tune-in to what kind of person it is whose birthday we are celebrating.

Doing the good deed . . . aah! Therein are the roots of Christmas joy.

The situations are endless in which Christmas love is needed and in which thoughtful helpfulness and genuine affection for others shape the joy of the day.

For example, convalescent institutions, prison cells, army camps, hospitals, centers for displaced and homeless persons, and nursing homes and the like have mushroomed across the country. What an opportunity to help, to spread Christmas, to do the Lord's work.

Christmas was trying to come into one extended-care center where my mother was a patient. The halls were swagged with kindergarten-like chains made in a therapy class by people with stricken bodies. Bows, bits of holly, and other adornments of the season were stuck to the pin-up boards by each room door. Christmas cards from loved ones who still remembered were taped above the hospital beds.

I came bearing a small tree and a shepherd set for my mother. Mother was in her ninetieth year and bedridden. Her brilliant mind was worn through and she had settled for events of the moment and not too many of those, either. Her condition was difficult; but on this day I learned an important truth: Mother's choice spirit was intact. True, it seemed buried beneath the burden of deterioration of the flesh, but was eternal!

It had been more than a week since I had been in town and I was trying to make up for it. I put the tree on the hospital table and arranged the shepherd and his lambs at the base, chirping along about this and that to Mother while I worked. I got no response from her. Not even the business of Christmas roused her. She was lost in her own vague world.

Overcome with the pity of it all, I cradled Mother in my arms, feeling like a child again, even though now I did the enveloping instead of Mother. Once you lose your mother you also lose this option, and it was only a short time later that my mother died.

Suddenly our tender moment was rudely interrupted. One of the "wanderers" from a room down the hall turned in through Mother's door and came to the bed where I crouched, holding mother in my arms.

The visitor crowded against us and flailed her arm between us. It was a jarring intrusion. I reacted accordingly, straightening up and staring in disbelief.

"Hug her! She needs you to love her." Mother slowly explained, gently pleading with me.

Mother's world was the nursing home now and narrow indeed. But her innate goodness was evident. She couldn't call me by my name, but she could still command my behavior. I did as she instructed, my heart swelling. Inside that poor body Mother lived! Seen or not, Christ lived and influenced! Christmas was come!

I think it would have been a satisfying contribution to have written such a fine piece of Christmas counsel as did Howard Thurmas for a Quaker calendar:

> When the song of the angel is stilled,
> When the star in the sky is gone,
> When the kings and princes are home,
> When the shepherds are back with their flock,
> The work of Christmas begins;

To find the lost,
To heal the broken,
To feed the hungry,
To release the prisoner,
To rebuild the nations,
To bring peace among brothers,
To make music in the heart.

And to hug the stranger at the nursing home, if that is what she aches for!

When we have celebrated Christmas in the way those lines suggest, we are heir to the great gifts God has promised us when we do his will. If we have done it unto the least we have done it unto the Savior. The words from Matthew 25:35–40 lend a grand, though simple, perspective to the season that has nothing to do with garlands and bells. The Lord speaks of the hungry, the thirsty, the stranger, the naked, the sick, the prisoners.

However, sometimes we take the words of Matthew too literally. We don't seem to know anyone who is hungry — overweight, yes, but starving no. Oh, we toss our canned goods for the needy onto the pile at the high school and we take our loaf to the shut-ins across the way. We take our poinsettias to the hospital. But the hungry, thirsty, homeless in our area? And surely there are no prisoners on our list of acquaintances.

But wait . . . one more story about the nursing home. We attended church services there, and sat at the back watching the sick and afflicted be shepherded in — wheeled, coaxed, bribed, and loudly spoken to, since most are deaf. It was a time of confusion. The patients sat in rows in an attitude of total disinterest or unawareness, babbling along non-stop through hymn, prayer, and the sacrament. In the row ahead of us were several silent ones, vacant eyed with dribbling lips.

Two young men from our home ward were passing the sacrament on that row, each starting at the aisle and working toward the center. One lad was a stalwart in all his young priesthood duties and in his personal life. The other was a rebel. He took part in Church activities only because his parents insisted. Or so it seemed. And yet how different his style was when passing the sacrament. While the stalwart youth ignored the patient who didn't reach for the sacrament, and moved on down the long row, the struggling youth was not content with that.

If the sacrament was worth passing, these people were supposed to take it. Time after time the young man would hold the tray and wait a few moments. If the patient didn't reach for the cup or the morsel, he would take the sacrament and gently force it into the mouth of the patient. Let it take whatever time was necessary, he'd persist, nudging the chin or cheek and separating the lips, if necessary.

Oh! It was wonderful! No Christmas message preached that day could touch the lesson I learned watching his compassionate, caring behavior.

This is the work of Christmas, remember. We have this burden: we who are commanded to feed the Lord's sheep, to lift the hands that hang down, and to relieve those less fortunate than we.

Surely many thirst for knowledge of how to live the gospel. Indeed many hunger among us for peace, a quiet conscience, comfort, and hope. What of the prisoners among us — those with addictive habits, difficult physical problems, constricting relationships, painful challenges. Also we have been warned that in the last days many Saints will be in financial bondage. Look about; do you know anyone who has been through the absolute agony of bankruptcy, for example?

A certain man had been unusually generous in sharing with those less comfortable than himself. Then circumstances occurred over a long period of time that finally forced him into the trauma of bankruptcy. He lost everything including the family home. Some people forgot his past generosities; but their friends came forward with an offer for housing to rent. When the word got out that the family now would be living in a fine home in another part of the neighborhood, a certain high priest said, "Well, *I* don't live in a home like that, and I'm not even bankrupt!"

It was meant to be funny and people laughed. However, the Spirit of Christ and the celebration of the season were forgotten. No joy, glad tidings, well wishing — just laughter.

Here was one in prison, for whatever cause. Someone else had come forth to provide housing for this stricken family while certain of their neighbors scoffed and questioned.

It reminds me of the old legend about the three who entered heaven on the same day. To interview them, the gatekeeper took each in turn. As each approached the gate, the gatekeeper asked, "What think ye of Christ?"

"Oh, I take cakes to the funerals, I line up the widows with the widowers, I help take down the chairs after meetings at the ward, I subscribe to the publications, and I pay for the manuals."

"Fine," said the gatekeeper. "Step right over here. Next."

And the second person approached the gate. "What think ye of Christ?"

"Oh! Chapter and verse and quote, quote, quote," spouted the zealot, reciting his memorized scriptures.

"I see. Step right over here, please. Next," said the gate-keeper.

"What think ye of Christ?" And the person fell at the feet of the gatekeeper and worshipped him.

You see, of course, that the first two meant well but didn't understand, while the third recognized the gatekeeper.

One of the often-ignored segments of the details of the first days of baby Jesus concerns the day Mary and Joseph took little Jesus to the temple to present him to God, after the custom of the law of the Jews. It is recorded in Luke that "there was one Anna, a prophetess: . . . she was of a great age, and had lived with an husband seven years from her virginity; and she was a widow of about fourscore and four years, which departed not from the temple, but served God" (Luke 2:36–37). And Anna was a woman who fasted and who prayed morning and night. This good woman recognized the infant in the temple as being the Son of God. So did Simeon. Observing the true spirit of Christmas, following after Christ himself, will help us to recognize the Savior and to recognize his blessings upon us when it is our turn.

The business of Christmas should be beyond mere jovial celebration and chic decor; beyond nostalgia and shallow sentiment. There should be ways in which we can implement the ideal into the icons of the season.

I am thinking now of nativity sets, for example. Many people have elaborate renderings of the manger scene, its animals, angels, wise men, shepherds, and shining star. They are so elegant, elaborate, and expensive that they are often left up all year long — as *objets d'art*, not as reminders of a proper philosophy of life. Perhaps the answer is to take a new look at our treasures of the season and to set standards by which to live according to what they represent. We can choose our music of the holidays with something more profound in mind than "I Saw Mama Kissing Santa Claus," and our reading material and gift giving could be on the level of soul enrichment.

It is a thought.

Tirelessly, each Christmas, our children moved the pieces of our nativity set back and forth across the crèche like checkers in a game, arranging and rearranging our manger scene with tenderness. It was our "Silent Night, Holy Night" scene that inevitably conjured up the spirit of that first Christmas into our home.

First Christmas — a telling phrase.

How well I recall our first Christmas in love when I received my diamond ring. Our first Christmas as newlyweds. Our first Christmas with Grandma in our home — her first as a widow. Our first Christmas in our new house with four little ones to play Santa for. Our first Christmas with a baby born at that time.

Then, full circle all too soon, it was our first Christmas alone together again.

I sat on the floor that Christmas with a small bundle of treasures of the shining season in my lap, loath to put them in place. Fingering each piece — the star, the angel, the ass — considering the symbol and remembering, I noted my mood swing from lonely reluctance at celebrating the day alone, to one of incredible anticipation.

The star. "And, lo, the star, which they saw in the east, went before them, till it came and stood over where the young child was." (Matthew 2:9.) I held up my star, mastercrafted in sterling silver, courtesy of the Metropolitan Museum of Art. It was an etched snowflake-like star that reminded me of the hundreds of New York youth who had presented it to me during their winterfest conference.

A star marked the place where Jesus was. A star gave the sign that he was near. People could be like the star. People could mark the place of the Savior, be his light — like those New York youth in the midst of a wicked world. This seasonal symbol was good all year.

Frankincense. This gum resin that comes from certain parts of the Holy Land. It is exotic, aromatic, and bright. It burns white and is long lasting. I opened the rude skin-envelope containing our own store of frankincense from our pilgrimage to Jerusalem. I caressed the lumps of this symbol of the gift of the Magi: "And [they] fell down, and worshipped him: and . . . presented unto him gifts; gold, and frankincense, and myrrh." (Matthew 2:11.)

Frankincense is another symbol for our lives. Stand ready and let the flame of worship be bright enough and long enough to make a difference to others. Remember the poet's comparison of a hero and a saint? The hero goes through the dark streets of life, lighting lamps for people to see by. The saint is himself a light. Ah, yes, to be a light. That is a proper gift to give Him.

Two turtledoves. These doves in my lap were of homespun cotton, hand embroidered by Guatemalan native women earning a coin for their keep. But why two turtledoves for Christmas — as a symbol for life? This scripture says "And when the days of her purification . . . were accomplished, they brought him to Jerusalem, to present him to the Lord, . . . and to offer a sacrifice, . . . a pair of turtledoves" (Luke 2:22, 24). This offering suggests the mission of Christ and *our* mission of sacrificing all that we have to help in the cause of the Lord. My turtledoves are a precious reminder.

The ass. In my lap was a donkey woven from straw in Mexico in a jaunty stance that primitive Mexican art lends creatures. Another donkey in another day carried Mary to Bethlehem. Another carried Christ into Jerusalem shortly before his crucifixion. "Thy king cometh unto thee, meek, and sitting upon an ass" (Matthew 21:5). This straw donkey reminded me that we should bear each other's burdens, meekly and in love. What is given to others is given to Him.

The angel. I stroked my angel, pitiful now with tarnished tinsel and its back scarred where wings had been sliced off in a teaching moment with my children long ago. This gift came from a choice friend when we were together in Podesta's Christmas Shop in San Francisco. I love this angel. It reminds me that I have lived!

The word *angel* comes from a root that means "messenger" or "instructor." Joseph was instructed by angels about Mary's condition. Angels instructed shepherds about prophecy and the fulfillment of promises, singing their good tidings of great joy that first Christmas.

The first Christmas meant joy at each stage of life under each circumstance as long as we were messengers of truth, too.

One can't go back, I realized afresh. But one can go forward.

The bundle of quaint Christmas treasures, symbols of the season, seemed to glow of its own light. Each piece lent a halo to the next. Looking at the items again, I remembered the lessons in the star, the beast of burden, the bright-burning resin, the angel; my happiness at that moment was greater than the sum of the symbols by far. They only stood for the roots of my joy.

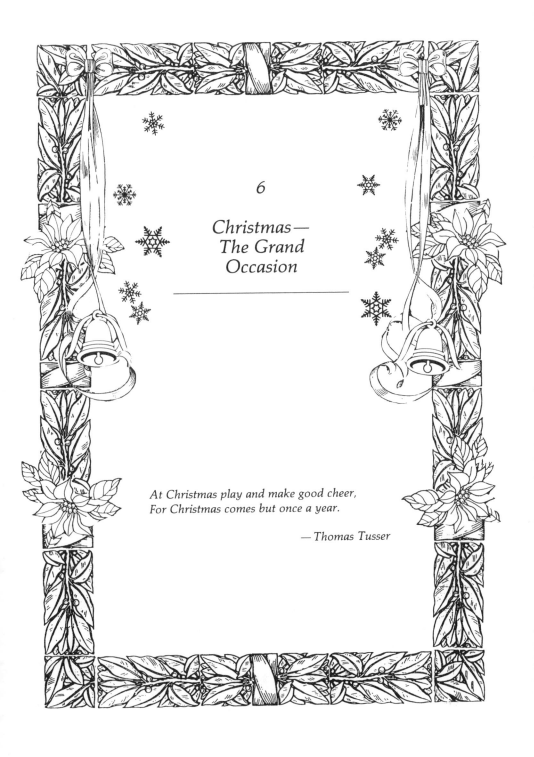

6

Christmas—
The Grand
Occasion

At Christmas play and make good cheer,
For Christmas comes but once a year.

— Thomas Tusser

6

Christmas—The Grand Occasion

Christmas is a grand occasion because people respond then, as at no other time, to the Spirit of the Christ whose birth on earth we celebrate.

Christmas is a grand occasion because of its good news, the glad tidings, the heralding angels with a presage of peace that we echo in our carols, our poetry, our stories, our decorations and our lifestyle for a season.

Christmas is a grand occasion because love reigns in the gatherings, the carolings, the honorings.

Christmas is a feeling, not just a calendar date. If the date comes and the feeling doesn't then the intent of it is lost. Going through the motions of Christmas isn't enough. Rising to the occasion and paying the price of proper pursuits of the season might be.

Christmas *is* a grand occasion—or it ought to be.

Such a grand occasion deserves our best efforts. The following suggestions might be helpful to your own celebration of the Sacred Birth:

1. *Traditions and Legends*
   The best traditions are the kind that let our hearts warm to

what the mind hasn't grasped yet. What loved ones feel together binds them in an eternal way.

Traditions have been defined as information, customs, and habits handed down from generation to generation, often via performances, without written instruction. Wouldn't it be wonderful if someone gave a family Christmas by writing down the family traditions and recording the instructions for the precious procedures that make a successful celebration for a certain family circle. Learn the legends of Christmas and weave them into the legends of the family, for example.

Where do our universal holiday traditions come from?

From the Hebrew Feast of Lights (or Dedication) come candles in profusion and in all sizes and shapes.

From the Druids comes the holly with its blood-red berries. They thought of it as the Savior's crown of thorns, and used it to ward off evil spirits.

From Britain comes the Yule log, a symbol in ancient Celtic times of celebration of the turning of the wheel of time.

From St. Boniface comes the use of a fir tree, "A living tree pointing to heaven." (Which may remind us to take another look at dead branches, metal cones, and artificial trees.)

From Nicholas of Lycia, who was present at the Council of Nice, a good and gift-giving man, comes the image of the jolly character known as St. Nicholas or Santa Claus.

From the far-northern countries of Scandinavia and Siberia come the sleigh and reindeer, tacked to the Santa legend by the Northern people when the St. Nicholas idea reached them.

From Germany come the carols, which often accompanied folk dances.

From the Holy Land comes the idea of gift giving reminiscent of the wise men and their gold, frankincense and myrrh.

From St. Francis of Assisi comes the crèche. Legend has it, that in A.D. 1223 he gathered real farm animals in a manger-like setting in the hope of stimulating people's imagination and appreciation for the Nativity. Then Italian artists began the production of crèche building and it flourished across Europe in following centuries.

And around the world all the commercial, colorful, light-studded, gift-laden, media-swollen, family-gathering, and emotion-ridden celebration came to be. With all the new and old symbols of the season, the trends, the foods, the changing styles of baubles and lights, comes a great and marvelous occasion. However simply or grandly it is conducted, it is because of the spirit of love and the eternal relationship of God and man that Christmas "happens."

2. *Say It Like It Is*

When you call a greeting of the season here's a choice — in any other language than your own it means warm wishes for best blessings!

God Jul	Swedish
Glædelig Jul	Danish
Gledelig Jul	Norwegian
Fröhliche Weihnachten	German
Hartelijke Kerst groeten	Dutch
Hauskaa Joulua	Finnish
Joyeux Noel	French
Buon Natale	Italian
Felice Navidad	Spanish
Boas Festas	Portuguese
S Rozhestvom Christova	Russian
Kala Christougenia	Greek
Linksmu Kaleou	Lithuanian
Chuk-syong Takn	Korean
Mele Kalikimaka	Hawaiian
Yasu Suntel Kowa	Chinese
Shin-nen Omeditō	Japanese

3. *Start a Tradition of Your Own*

Some have a stranger in. Some sub for Santa. Some have a well-wishing party for the children in a rehab center or pediatric ward of the local hospital. Some invite neighbors to come into the home and explain their own traditions of the season. "For still will Christmas gild the year's mischances," and understanding comes at last among people of different faith.

Memories linked with sight, smell, sound, scent, touch, and taste last longer. Down the years they are easily triggered by a glimpse, a whiff, a tune, a crumb.

4. *Use the Symbols of Christmas*

Snowflakes have become symbols of Christmas, too, along with hearts and candles, prickly wreaths or crowns of thorns, angels, manger scenes, and stars. Use the symbols of Christmas to teach valuable truths.

One Christmas my family had moved into a home that desperately needed somebody's tender-loving care, but only after the holidays could we redecorate. So I gathered our children around me and explained that this was one year when they could turn every window they wanted into a winter wonderland of snowflakes. I talked about God's miracle of snowflakes, each unique (as people are). Alike, yes, but different from each other.

We folded type paper and snipped the duplicating designs. We unfolded the paper flakes and voila! Beauty! Some were more intricate than others, depending on the age of the snipping child. But to each his own was loveliest. Then we taped the flakes to the window as stencils, using snow spray to make each pane of glass a winter flake. Suddenly our home was that winter wonderland we Northerners like for our Christmas holidays.

Remember, the miracles of God are represented by the intricate, individualistic snowflakes. And remember, too, the healing, lifting, delightful miracles in life because of certain choice relationships!

One year we rounded up the grandchildren and great-grandchildren of George Q. Cannon, my husband's grandfather, and went to each home of the remaining first-generation children of President Cannon to sing them our greetings for a merry, merry Christmas. One of the aunts in her late eighties was delightful in her surprise. She clapped her hands together as she opened the door of her little apartment and saw all of her younger relatives. "Somebody knows I am alive!" she cried. "I know it now, too."

A favorite game that one family plays on Christmas Eve is to gather the children (and everyone finally ends up being a child before the game is finished) in a circle on the floor, each child standing in front of one member of the extended family, who leads them through a traditional Christmas ritual. The nativity scene is on the grown-up's lap. One by one, an animal from the manger is held up before the children, and the children sing about what that animal says when it gets up in the morning.

"When lambs get up in the morning, they always say good day. Baa! Baa! Baa! Baa! That is what they say."

The children then sing through the donkey, the cow, the duck, the dog, and the chickens. The crowning verse comes when the leader holds up the angel, lately perched on the roof of the manger behind the star. "When angels get up in the morning, they always say good day, Alleluia! Allelulia! That is what they say."

Many families hold the manger scene as a major part of the birthday celebration for the baby Jesus. The manger marked Christ's beginning and symbolized his uniqueness. Our son's family carries this tradition over into the celebration of the birthdays of their own children. Instead of displaying the manger scene used for Christ's birthday, they mount pictures and memorabilia about the birthday child on the bulletin board. The accompanying remarks state, "Christ was born in a manger. Where were you born?" And with these comparisons the connection is made.

A small Christmas sock filled with fragrant pine needles is annual joy when this treasure is brought from the storage box. The container can be needlepointed, quilted, embroidered together with ribbons and packed with satin, tapestried, made of velvet, appliquéd or stitched, knitted, or designed with iron-on tape. The idea is to make a charming storage place for a sprinkle of needles that are taken from the greens each season and saved for another year when they can be hung for nostalgia and a spice scent.

Since Christmas Eve is the special time, a grand buffet at 5:00 P.M. is perfect for gathering loved ones into the spirit. It is an enchanting time of anticipation and secrets. The buffet spread on the eve is a hearty welcoming to invited lonely ones, guests, drop-ins, and gracious carolers. What a send-off for the celebration. And the cooking for Christmas Day is already done!

A candlelight supper of the soup (or rarebit, fondu,

quiche?) you make only at Christmas every year stirs memories of other suppers at Christmas. A Danish sweet dough baked in a wreath becomes part of the tradition.

For eager children, breakfast can come in a special Christmas lunch box, or even in a Santa sock stuffed with mini sweet rolls, orange wedges tipped with powdered sugar, dates rolled in sugar and boasting a pecan center, deviled eggs, and a small bag of home-flavored cereal snacks. And they can be made ahead! Let children with scrubbed hands squiggle the breadsticks and dip them in butter and parmesan cheese before arranging and arranging and arranging them on the baking sheet. They'll find their treats to eat in their breakfast box.

On the other hand, breakfast might be the production at your house. It could be The Works, including French chocolate, deviled eggs in swiss-cheese sauce with chopped fresh parsley and pimento, and dollar-sized hot cakes or enormous cinnamon buns with glazing drizzled in a tree shape. Behind every wreathed door is a different menu, but the fare remains the same each year in each house!

Some families have a wake-up parade. The first one up Christmas morning chooses a family member to awaken with the greeting, "We wish you a Merry Christmas!" After the mock protestations are over, the two then go to a third person who joins the parade. When all are gathered they sing as they march to the tree with the gifts.

Tender Trappings

A hand-painted masterpiece from a hand-crafted pine box and lid is a treasure for each of our sibling family units. The family of each of our children uses their box in a different way but always give it a prominent place as a Christmas tradition. Into storage go precious tree ornaments and memorabilia of the season, like the nativity sets, the potpourri jar, the crystal tree for holding mints, the music boxes, the garlands. Our stores contain the rhythm band instruments to accompany the caroling.

Some families have Christmas surprise-balls. This has long been our family's favorite happening as the last event on Christmas night. We'd make those surprise-balls ahead to be ready for

Christmas, a great summer project at the vacation home. They are time consuming but well worth it. Each ball is made by wrapping strips of various colors of crepe paper into a ball, securing tiny trinkets within the wrappings.

When the ball is the size of a big orange, the loose end is glued into place. Then the artistry of turn-a-ball-into-a-friend takes places as facial expressions distinguish one ball from another. Hats, ribbons, eyelashes, beards, a scarf, an Indian feather, yarn pigtails, stiff or ruffled collars, kerchief or shawl, flower or spectacles all add personality to the "Christmas friends." Then, on Christmas night, the strips of crepe paper are unwound, the trinkets are found, and the squeals of delight from adults as well as children top off the day.

One family entertains little guests at a cookie-shine party. While our daughter-in-law Becky shapes and bakes her special sugar-cookie recipe, the fifteen or twenty children sit at their posts, around pots of colored frosting, candy drops, shredded coconut, and cake-decorating tubes filled with icing. Each has a plate on which to store his or her finished star, candy-cane, elfin, angel, Santa, and teddy-bear cookie creations. Dad takes pictures and samples. It is the social event of their children's Christmas.

Win Jardine has been baking Christmas braids on Christmas Eve for forty-five years. After all the baking and frosting and tie-up with holly sprig is finished the Jardine family drives to the homes of special friends and carols as they offer their gift for Christmas breakfast. Wonderful!

Another family worked together to make colorful costumes for the nativity cast. These were simple, shapeless and sizeless but sacred to all because of the characters they depict. Each year, shepherds, wise men, Joseph, Mary, and the baby Jesus would be played by different people but they would wear the traditional costumes. Costume suppliers, craft houses, and the neighborhood variety store offered multitudes of choices for turning a sheet into swaddling clothes, a bath towel into a Jerusalem shepherd's robe. Each season the costumes are gently removed from storage and assigned to a new cast who dons them with reverence as well as excitement. Each finale includes ceremoniously removing the costumes and carefully folding them into a Christmas box for safe keeping until the next baby Jesus Birthday Party on Christmas Eve. The family member who directs the production gives a little talk about protecting the costumes and about who else has worn them through the years. Such a rewarding tradition.

Another family had a professional come to their home before Christmas one year to show them how to cover loose-leaf binders with Christmas fabric and designs. Then these Christmas Eve books were filled with material to be read aloud together on Christmas Eve — the scriptural references that tell the holy story; the carols; favorite Christmas legends and poetry. And a reading of the "minutes" of the preceding year's celebration is a favorite part of their Christmas book.

Lights On

It has been said that the eyes are the windows to the soul. Christmas is all about soul.

Light up your eyes to match the sparkling winter skies. Light up your eyes to match the lights on your tree, in your windows, around your wreath, on your mantel, on your hearth, in the bare-leafed trees that reflect in shadowed snow.

Let your eyes light up as you react to the scene and moods of the season. Mentally and spiritually prepare to add joy to the season by being a light yourself. Respond in kindness to the efforts and goodness of others, old and young, friend or family or stranger, within your gate. No casual gesture or mumbled "thanks" will do for you!

Light up your eyes and turn on that smile as you try more than ever before to follow the teachings and example of Christ this special day.

Light up your eyes as you help carry the inevitable burdens of preparation. The little ones have their concerns about Santa and grown-ups have their Santa concerns. Maybe you can be the one with time and inclination to create moods, to merry up the making of the season.

Characteristics of Christmas

It is characteristic of Christmas to do unto others as you would have others do unto you. Generously give whatever you can; thoroughly forgive, striving to overcome estrangements; and diligently remember the ones so easily forgotten: the service people, shopkeepers, tot tenders, book lenders, crossing guards, postal carriers, volunteer workers, church leaders, and paper boys.

The bishopric in a ward we lived in, woke up on Valentine's morning to find their gardens and lawns sprouting hearts, colorful paper hearts telling the world that the youth in their ward loved them. It is a great idea that would work just as well at Christmas using pop-up stars, earth fallen but joy bringing!

Finnish people carpet the graves of their loved ones with paper sacks cut in designs to reveal lighted candles within. What a sight! This is a charming tradition, with each family carrying one as they make a trek to the resting place of their ancestors. It lights the season as well as the graves.

Youth-group activities and family gatherings held long before Christmas provide ready labor for the happy tasks of turning bushel baskets into gift totes, of preparing origami cones or cups to hold treats for visiting children, and of making colorful catch-alls from huge grocery sacks for discarded gift wrappings. These creations will burn in the fireplace with proper ceremony after all the unwrapping is done. It makes clean up more fun than chore.

For friends you can leave a Yule log — boasting sparklers, pine cones, and net bags of cinnamon or clove — fragrantly burning. Children love to help prepare a winter bird tree decorated with bits of suet, croutons, bacon, cheese, raisins, orange peel, and yarn. Oh, a winter bird tree makes lovely watching during all the dark days after Christmas!

Mary Webb wrote, ". . . I was glad of what I had, as a winter bird is, that will come into your hand for a little crumb, though in plenteous times she would but mock you from the topmost bough. I took my crumb, and behold! it was the Lord's Supper." (Mary Webb, *Precious Bane*.)

One of our neighbor families shared a fat packet of their favorite home-mix for hot chocolate. The cocoa and sugar had spices added that marked it for Christmas comfort.

Others prepared fire starts for the home hearth made in Christmas shapes from tallow. Like small flat candles, they contain wicks and are ready to flame up the logs at the touch of a match. And at Christmas, when you light that fire of yours, let there be in your heart at each dancing flame a song of remembrance.

When the children are done with their nativity play, the adults in a certain family have a segment of their own. One of the women plays Elisabeth, one of the men plays her husband, Zacharias, and another man plays the nephew, Benjamin. Their conversation was created by gifted Clinton Larson:

Elisabeth: Benjamin, my nephew, that, and more. I have seen Mary before as a child, but now the wonder of motherhood is upon her, her solemn eyes and the grace of her walk. Zacharias, she has changed! How can I be what I have been, the dour advisor of youth for the holiness of the Talmud? She holds the wisdom of the leaf for which the tree was made, and the blossom, in the moment of the natural glory that we feel when the season of waiting is no more, and the color of spring appears, and the air glistens with the scent of the willows by the river and the song of the wren. The blossoms tremble, the times open on the meadows of Canaan, and the promise is here! (She looks up.)

Help me, Zacharias. I must be standing!

(There is a sound from the roadway. Zacharias goes to her and helps her up.)

Elisabeth: Thank you, my husband. Hold me for a moment. I can hardly stand, I am trembling so!

Benjamin: I have never seen you this way before.

Elisabeth: (In a rapture): Go! Go! Tell me what you see!

(Benjamin goes to the gate and looks down the road.)

Benjamin: Yes, it is! It is Joseph and Mary! They are with her parents!

Elisabeth: Come with me, Zacharias. Is my robe straight? My hair? (Zacharias goes to her, perplexed and wondering.) Your arm. Zacharias, it is the mother of the Lord!

The Essence of Christmas

Jesus the Christ was born of a virgin and we mark the season as Christmas. Later he was cruelly martyred on a cross, and was resurrected, an occasion we now celebrate as Easter. Those who love Jesus celebrate these important events in reverence as well as joy. Whatever the traditions of this grand occasion at your house, the celebration might be done in gratitude as well. The guide for what we do might be taken more from what *he* did while he lived on earth among men for thirty-three years. Then Christmas would truly be a grand occasion.

Let's consider again the beloved portion of the Christmas story as recorded in Luke 2:1—16:

> And it came to pass in those days, that there went out a decree from Ceasar Augustus, that all the world should be taxed.
>
> (And this taxing was first made when Cyrenius was governor of Syria.)
>
> And all went to be taxed, every one into his own city.
>
> And Joseph also went up from Galilee, out of the city of Nazareth, into Judaea, unto the city of David, which is called Bethlehem; (because he was of the house and lineage of David:)
>
> To be taxed with Mary his espoused wife, being great with child.
>
> And so it was, that, while they were there, the days were accomplished that she should be delivered.
>
> And she brought forth her firstborn son, and wrapped him in swaddling clothes, and laid him in a manger; because there was no room for them in the inn.
>
> And there were in the same country shepherds abiding in the field, keeping watch over their flock by night.
>
> And, lo, the angel of the Lord came upon them, and the glory of the Lord shone round about them: and they were sore afraid.
>
> And the angel said unto them, Fear not: for behold, I bring you good tidings of great joy, which shall be to all people.
>
> For unto you is born this day in the city of David a Saviour, which is Christ the Lord.
>
> And this shall be a sign unto you; Ye shall find the babe wrapped in swaddling clothes, lying in a manger.
>
> And suddenly there was with the angel a multitude of the heavenly host praising God, and saying,

Glory to God in the highest, and on earth peace, good will toward men.

And it came to pass, as the angels were gone away from them into heaven, the shepherds said one to another, Let us now go even unto Bethlehem, and see this thing which is come to pass, which the Lord hath made known unto us.

And they came with haste, and found Mary, and Joseph, and the babe lying in a manger.

7

Glad Tidings
of Christmas

I heard a bird sing
In the dark of December,
A magical thing
And sweet to remember —
We are nearer to spring
Than we were in September,
I heard a bird sing
In the dark of December.

7

Glad Tidings of Christmas

T he quaint lines "I heard a bird sing" express the side of Christmas that Jesus brought to all mankind. They speak of months and seasons of the year, but they are the poet's gift to us about the glorious hope that filled the earth with the coming of the Christ child.

My husband and I took a trip with friends to the birthplace of Jesus. We watched the sun set over Bethlehem and for a few moments that little city on the hill was radiant with color bouncing off its quaint skyline. Then in waning light the evening star appeared. It was only a few weeks before the time when we celebrate the Savior's birth, and from our stony seat on Shepherd's Hill we marveled at the star's size, at its commanding brightness as it hung low over Bethlehem. This star marked for us the place where Jesus was born. Artist Floyd Breinholt caught this scene on film for each of us to enjoy during all of our Christmastimes thereafter.

And then, the unique *clinkle* of Holy Land livestock-bells announced an age-old parade. We saw a shepherd, in robes that have changed little in over two thousand years, leading his bleating lambs across those plains shortly below us. We were awestruck with the timing. It was as if we were witnessing a replay of the precious happening two thousand years ago on that silent night when Christ was born—that holy night when the angel of the Lord came upon the wondering shepherds who knew the usual night sky and who marveled at the new star. The glory of the Lord shone round about these shepherds and "they were sore afraid" as the angel spoke to them. "Fear not: for, behold, I bring you good tidings of great joy, which shall be to all people." The angel explained how to find the newborn king, "And suddenly there was with the angel a multitude of the heavenly hosts praising God, and singing. 'Glory to God in the highest and on earth peace, good will toward men.' " (Luke 2:9—14.)

Sitting there we contemplated the meaning of such glad tidings in our own lives until suddenly this latter-day multitude of Saints gathered on Shepherd's Hill took up the herald of the angels and sang with increasing unison and emotion evoked by an even surer awareness of the miracle of Bethlehem: "Far, far away on Judea's plains . . . glory to God . . . peace on earth, good-will . . . peace on earth . . ."

We read, then, the final lines of the story of the first Christmas with new understanding. The shepherds "returned" from worshipping the babe in swaddling clothes and they praised God to all who would listen. The wise men came to Jesus with gifts of gold, frankincense, and myrrh. For *his* protection they departed for home another way.

Nothing would ever be the same again for the wise men, for the shepherds, or for any of us who had made a pilgrimage— through travel or through study—to be near the Lord Jesus.

Since the beginning people have tried to express their feelings about these sacred events about their love for Jesus and their hope of life in the peace that comes from being near to him. In this chapter we include a careful selection of glad tidings.

In Bethlehem, a young mother had purchased a crèche of hand-carved olive wood. The next Christmas when the lovely figures of the scene of the first Christmas were brought forth from their wrappings, they seemed to shine for her. Here in her own home was a treasure, a portion of Bethlehem. She was moved to write a prayer that is now recited each Christmas when the family has finished setting up this Bethlehem crèche and the other manger scenes that they have collected over the years:

Bless this wooden stable, Lord. This lowly abode of cows and donkeys. May it keep me humble this Christmas.

Bless this tiny star beaming at the top. May it light my eyes with the wonder of Your caring.

Bless the little angel. May her song glow through our house and fill it with smiles.

Bless this caring shepherd and the small lamb cradled in his arms. May it whisper of Your caring embrace on my life.

Bless these Wise Men bearing splendid gifts. May they inspire me to lay my shining best at Your feet.

Bless this early father in his simple robe. May he remind me of all You have entrusted to my care.

Bless this Virgin Mother. May she teach me patience as I tend to my own little ones.

And bless this Baby nestled in the hay. May the love He brought to earth that Bethlehem night so fill my heart with compassion and warmth that it becomes a Christmas gift to those around me." (Sue Monk Kidel, "The Blessing of the Crèche." Excerpted with permission from *Guideposts Magazine*. Copyright © 1981 by Guideposts Associates, Inc., Carmel, NY 10512.)

Among the various glad tidings that countless writers and speakers have expressed in exuberant reactions to the season, surely we can find something among them that says it like Christmas is for us!

Like Christina Rossetti's wise worry about Christmas giving, "What Can I Give Him?" We had Marsha Fox prepare the following lines in her inimitable calligraphy. Then we framed the masterpiece, mounted it at the base of a small tree decorated with red foil-wrapped chocolate hearts, and used it as a desk decoration in the Church's Young Women offices. It was a charming reminder of what Christmas giving can be.

> What can I give Him
> Poor as I am?
> If I were a shepherd,
> I would give Him a lamb,
> If I were a Wise Man
> I would do my part, —
> Yet what I can I give Him,
> Give my heart.

Henry Wadsworth Longfellow had something to say about giving, an element of Christmas that harks back to the wise men: "Give what you have. To someone, it may be better than you dare to think." Peter and James at the temple gate gave what they had. To the beggar asking for alms, Peter said, "Silver and gold have I none; but such as I have give I thee: In the name of Jesus Christ of Nazareth rise up and walk." (Acts 3:6.) And he did. Now, that was a gift!

Old Phoenix Jackson didn't have silver and gold, either. But what she had she gave with all her heart. Phoenix is the heroine of the short story, "A Worn Path," by Eudora Welty. Her story touches me at this season, especially. Hers was a mighty effort though a small deed. Yet what a difference it made. Her story reminds us of how much we have to be grateful for: the period in which we live, the places we are when we learn our lessons, the comforts we enjoy even when we're stricken.

It was December — a bright frozen day in the early morning. Far out in the country there was an old negro woman with her head tied in a red rag, coming along a path through the pinewoods. Her name was Phoenix Jackson. She was very old and small and she walked slowly in the dark pine shadows, moving a little from side to side in her steps, with the balanced heaviness and lightness of a pendulum in a Grandfather clock. She carried a thin, small cane made from an umbrella, and with this she kept tapping the frozen earth in front of her. This made a grave and persistent noise in the still air, that seemed meditative, like the chirping of a solitary little bird . . . parting her way from side to side with the cane, through the whispering field; at last she came to a wagon track, where the silver grass blew between the red ruts . . . suddenly over she went in the ditch, like a little puff of milk-weed and she couldn't get up. A white man finally came along and found her—a hunter, a young man, with his dog on a chain.

"Well, Granny!" he laughed. "What are you doing there?"

"Lying on my back like a June-bug waiting to be turned over, mister," she said, reaching up her hand.

"Anything broken, Granny?"

"No sir, them old dead weeds is springy enough," said Phoenix when she had got her breath . . .

"On your way home?"

"No sir, I going to town."

"Why, that's too far! That's as far as I walk when I come out myself. Now you go on home, Granny!"

"I bound to go to town, mister," said Phoenix. "The time come around."

The man left and Phoenix found a nickel that had fallen from his jacket as he stooped to lift her up. She put it in her pocket and trudged on, reaching town at last. Moving slowly from side to side, she went into a stone building and into a tower of steps, where she walked up and around and around until her feet knew to stop.

She entered a door, and announced,

"Here I be." There was a fixed and ceremonial stiffness over her body.

The nurse wanted to know about Phoenix's grandson who had swallowed lye two or three years before. She wondered if the boy were any better than the last time Phoenix came for medicine—or if he were dead.

"No, missy, he not dead, he just the same, every little while his throat begin to close up again, and he not able to swallow. He not get his breath. He not able to help himself. So the time come around, and I go on another trip for the soothing medicine . . . my little grandson, he sit up there in the house all wrapped up, waiting by himself. We is the only two left in the world. He suffer and it don't seem to put him back at all. He got a sweet look. He going to last. He wear a little patch quilt and peep out, holding his mouth open like a little bird . . . I could tell him from all the others in creation."

"All right." The nurse was trying to hush her now. She brought her a bottle of medicine. "Charity," she said, making a mark in a book. Old Phoenix held the bottle close to her eyes and then carefully put it into her pocket.

"I thank you," she said.

"It's Christmas time, Grandma," said the attendant. "Could I give you a few pennies out of my purse?"

"Five pennies is a nickel," said Phoenix stiffly.

"Here's a nickel," said the attendant.

Phoenix rose carefully and held out her hand. She received the nickel and then fished the other nickel out of her pocket and laid it beside the new one. She stared at her palm closely, with her head on one side.

Then she gave a tap with her cane on the floor.

"This is what come to me to do," she said. "I going to the store and buy my child a little windmill they sells, made out of paper. He going to find it hard to believe there such a thing in the world. I'll march myself back where he waiting, holding it straight up in this hand."

She lifted her free hand, gave a little nod, turned round and walked out of the doctor's office. Then her slow step began on the stairs, going down. (Excerpted from *A Curtain of Green and Other Stories*, Harcourt, Brace World, Inc.)

I think it was Thoreau who said, "We do not need for friends to feed and clothe our bodies — neighbors are kind enough for that — but to do the like office for our spirits." Like Phoenix! Not many of us will be put to the test old Phoenix had, nor can we do what Christ did for us. Surely, though, with all we have, each of us can give something. With all that has gone wrong out there in the world, with all that is making hearts break around us, we can put comfort into Christmas!

"I am thinking of you today because it is Christmas" wrote Henry Van Dyke. "And I wish you happiness. And tomorrow, because it will be the day after Christmas, I shall still wish you happiness. My thoughts and my wishes will be with you always. Whatever joy comes to you will make me glad. All through the year . . . I wish you the spirit of Christmas."

These are my sentiments exactly. Now, consider these tender lines that every mother will understand.

> They all were looking for a king
> To slay their foes and lift them high;
> Thou cam'st, a little baby thing
> That made a woman cry.
>
> —George Macdonald

How many old recollections and how many dormant sympathies Christmastime awakens within us. Some of the best literature, most appealing poetry, and most popular seasonal movies deal with feelings that naturally well up in our hearts about home — childhood home, too — and loved ones, friends, and familiar objects. They depict traditions that aren't so important in and of themselves, but which remind us of the healing warmth and charity that we feel about others who share the season with us by design, by choice, or by circumstance.

We are indebted to Dickens again and again for saying it for us:

> We write those words now, many miles distant from the spot at which, year after year, we met in that day, a merry and joyous circle. Many of the hearts that throbbed so gaily then have ceased to beat; and yet the old house, the room, the merry voices and smiling faces, the jest, the laugh, the most minute and trivial circumstance connected with those happy meetings, crowd upon our mind at each recurrence of the season, as if the last assemblage had been but yesterday. Happy, happy Christmas, that can win us back to the delusions of our childish days, recall to the old man the pleasures of his youth, and transport the traveler back to his own fireside and quiet home!
>
> —Charles Dickens

Welcome! all Wonders in one sight!
    Eternity shut in a span.
Summer in winter, day in night,
    Heaven in earth, and God in man.
Great little one! whose all-embracing birth
    Lifts earth to heaven, stoops heav'n to earth!
                —Richard Crashaw

You have heard of the "Twelve Days of Christmas," an old English carol for the twelve days between Christmas and Epiphany? Well, here's *my* variation on that theme: "The Twelve *Ways* of Christmas."

Now, the first way of Christmas is the Message we all love of the Babe born in Bethlehem of old.

The second way of Christmas is Music — carols, bells and the herald angels' hymn of praise to God.

Now, the third way of Christmas is People, real and fancied, who give meaning and memory to the day.

The fourth way of Christmas is Parties, fun galore; goodies on the table and guests at the door.

The fifth way of Christmas is Creativity with the whole family decking halls and crèche, mantel, tree.

The sixth way of Christmas is Customs-Traditions — from the way the stockings hang to the star we all envision.

The seventh way of Christmas is Prayer this holy day.

The eighth way of Christmas is Gifts in bright array.

The ninth way of Christmas is Giving graciously and thanking all concerned enthusiastically.

The tenth way of Christmas is Stories that we tell — Dickens, Luke and Clements Moore and current ones as well.

The eleventh way of Christmas is Poetry, remembered verse and greeting cards and tender "masterpiece."

The twelfth way of Christmas is Spirit that we feel of joy and hope and confidence in Christ the Prince of Peace.

It is pleasant — even wise — to be a child at Christmastime; Jesus was, whose birthday we celebrate! To be joy makers and joy bringers and joy feelers at Christmas is a blessing for others. Blessed are the joy bringers!

Michael Moody's family always sings an original carol. It's a tradition for Michael to put poet Mabel Jones Gabbott's newest Christmas poem to music. And each is wonderful, wonderful! We're including here the one from 1979 called *Sleep Little Jesus.*

There are many precious poems and many treasured stories themed to the Christmas celebration. Each is the way one person perceives Christmas. Here is a selection of some that have meant Christmas to me over the years. They can add to your own perspective about this holiday season.

GENTLE JESUS

Words by Mabel Jones Gabbott

Music by Michael F. Moody

1. Gen - tle Je - sus in the man - ger Came to teach us all to care For each oth - er, for the stran - ger, Came to show us love and prayer.

2. Gen - tle Je - sus, Ho - ly Ba - by, Born in lit - tle Beth - le - hem. Shep - herds brought their gifts to praise him, Ma - gi left him pre - cious gems.

3. Gen - tle Je - sus in the star - light, Heav'n - ly an - gels sang his birth. Gen - tle Je - sus in the sta - ble, Lord of heav'n and Lord of earth.

This song may be performed as a piano duet by playing the melody up an octave.

"Not believe in Santa Claus? You might as well not believe
in fairies . . . No Santa Claus! Thank God, he lives and he lives
forever. A thousand years from now, Virginia, nay, ten times
ten-thousand years from now, he will continue to make glad the
heart of childhood."

—Francis Parcellus Church

Giovanni's Gifts

There is nothing I can give you
which you have not; but there is much, very much,
that while I cannot give it, you can take.

No heaven can come to us unless our hearts
find rest in today. Take heaven!
No peace lies in the future which is not hidden
in the present. Take peace!
The gloom of the world is but a shadow.
Behind it, yet within our reach, is joy. Take joy!

Life is so full of meaning and purpose,
so full of beauty — beneath its covering —
that you will find earth but cloaks your heaven.

And so at this Christmas time, I greet you.
Not quite as the world sends greetings,
but with profound esteem and with the prayer
that for you, now and forever,
the day breaks and the shadows flee away.

—Fra Giovanni da Fiesole

Why do the bells of Christmas ring?
Why do little children sing?
Once a lovely shining star,
Seen by shepherds from afar,
Gently moved until its light
Made a manger's cradle bright.
There a darling baby lay,
Pillowed soft upon the hay,
And its mother sang and smiled:
"This is Christ, the Holy Child!"

Therefore the bells for Christmas ring,
Therefore little children sing.

—Eugene Field

Then all the Cratchit family drew round the hearth, in what Bob Cratchit called a circle . . . and at Bob Cratchit's elbow stood the family display of glass. Two tumblers and a custard-cup without a handle.

These held the hot stuff from the jug, however, as well as golden goblets would have done; and Bob served it with beaming looks, while the chestnuts on the fire sputtered and cracked noisily. Then Bob proposed:

"A Merry Christmas to us all, my dears. God bless us!"

"God bless us every one!" said Tiny Tim, the last of all.

—Charles Dickens

Over the years since, Bob Cratchit's Christmas toast has become the perfect and favorite greeting among friends celebrating the beloved season.

8

Christmas— A Blessing

May the blessed light be on you,
light without and light within.
May the blessed sunlight shine on you
and warm your heart until
it glows like a great fire,
so that a stranger may come
and warm himself at it,
and also a friend.
May God always bless you,
love you, and keep you.

8

Christmas—A Blessing

ome say that the ancient blessing or wish for the season that introduces this chapter is the essence of a happy holiday.

Some say that people "talk of Christmas so long that it comes!" We say, "Let it! Look at the blessings it brings." It carries with it reunions with loved ones and opportunities for healing estranged relationships. It stirs remembrances so treasured they're worth more than money or the things money can buy. Christmas is replete with reminders of happy possibilities both present and future. It is a time in which we can recharge our spiritual batteries, become more devoted disciples of Christ, and feel fresh, reverent tenderness for the trio of the Nativity: Mary, the mother of the son of God; the noble stepfather Joseph; and Jesus, the innocent infant born to a life of sacrifice and exquisite pain in shouldering the sins of this world.

Some say that when Jesus was born the sun danced in the sky. Leaves burst forth on bare trees, and fruit ripened out of season. Gnarled olive trees straightened, and voiceless birds sang. All animals were domesticated for a time. Cripples walked and the blind could see. All natural affections were evident among God's children. Such was the wonder of change at his coming to earth.

Our own lives feel freshened and ripened as Christmas works its magic. Year after year we are anxious and willing partakers of the celebration. We stand a little straighter ourselves before our ugly burdens. We sprout qualities we weren't sure we had. There are hints of majesty in our souls. We even deal splendidly with our fellows. No person is an enemy, only troubled. Compassion and mercy come to us more easily and we hope against hope we can behave better longer this season than ever before.

I first became aware of the importance of dealing splendidly with others at Christmas at least, one wintry day as I sat by the small brick-arched fireplace in our Wall Street home. I was watching the lumps of bituminous coal glow into embers. I was thinking about what I had read in a new book that I had received for Christmas. It was Dale Carnegie's *How to Win Friends and Influence People.* Santa was always trying to help me and this time it worked. I had a new insight about giving and getting.

Carnegie talked about being a people pleaser. It was a new dimension on the old golden-rule principle of treating others as you'd like to be treated that interested me. Carnegie said that if you are going fishing, you want to catch fish. So you don't take your own favorite food for bait. You don't expect fish to jump to the bait of strawberries and cream, for example. You take worms.

So, if you want to win friends, I interpreted, you don't feed people your own favorite things: you feed them theirs! Great!

You don't *just* treat others as you yourself like to be treated; you treat others as *they* like to be treated. That goes for gifts, compliments, conversations, and love.

Caught in the spell of this good will toward men, I learned to hedge on truth at Christmas. I just couldn't bear to see anyone disenchanted at Christmas, not the giver of the gift nor the recipient. And the year after the gift of Carnegie, I girded up my Christmas spirit and hugged my grandmother warmly, thanking her for the old-fashioned hand-crocheted doilies I thought I'd never use. Over the Christmases I collected something like thirty of them. When my mother died an old woman, I marked the occasion by giving one of these doilies, made by her mother for me, to each of her granddaughters with an accompanying legend. Now they are coveted and grace pillows, hang framed on walls and mark the folder for temple clothes. Tender reminders of heritage. If I had turned off the gift of doilies early on . . .

I remember applying this lesson years later when I told myself I liked the crude broom-handle boot drier made by my young husband. It was exactly what I had longed for always! It was the thought that counted, you know, and though this item didn't seem to require much thought, I knew it was a labor of love for my husband because he was not born to be a carpenter! Each of us has given or received such gifts. Spiritual maturity increases the value of such a gift beyond anything money could buy.

This principle worked in me in such a way that I would not allow myself to admit disappointment when Santa's surprises were surveyed. I believed in the system. As soon as you stop "believing" you get pajamas or underwear instead. Surprise! Even at its worst, Christmas was better than any other day of the year. Still, it could be made even better if people would only try a little harder or learn a little more about human relationships, about gratitude, and about how God's love for us should be transmitted into our love for others.

When I was a girl, an annual tradition Christmas morning consisted of our neighborhood's gang of girls parading up and down the blocks to see what each had found beneath her tree. How parents permitted such an abomination of the day, such a trial-by-comparison trauma, I can't understand. Child psychology hadn't reached Capitol Hill homes in those days, I suppose, but surely the golden rule had! At any rate, the parade persisted, year after year, and the pain of the day went with it.

The gifts beneath the trees in the homes of my friends were as different as their incomes and situations, as different as their parents' tastes and concerns for the celebration allowed. These differences and comparisons always brought pain for somebody. What people received for Christmas neither declared their own happiness nor determined their popularity (a term we used frequently then and which, in our circle, was practically synonymous with happiness). You see, the girl whose family was hardest hit in the Depression received the least for Christmas. But she was the most popular. And the girl who got too much suffered one more rejection.

That's how I learned to hedge the whole truth at Christmas. My heart would break.

One Christmas we traipsed into the home of the girl who always got too much. We entered, surveyed, and gasped. Gift after gift was shown to us. When she finally displayed the little pearl ring in a velvet box, we all just looked away. You can't eat pearls and they won't keep you warm, and that was what gift giving was all about in those times.

But this girl felt rejected, and the Christmas light went out in her eyes at our response. My child's heart tightened with the snap of the lid of the velvet ring box.

"It's beautiful," I said. That was no lie. But then I continued, "I wish I had one, too."

That last part was the lie. I said it not out of greed nor envy, but out of good will. I had hoped to give her a friend, but the ring was the final blow that set her apart from the others. The ring was too much, too marvelous, and it made her someone the other girls couldn't understand or ever be.

There was a friend in that pitiful Christmas parade whose father gave her a pair of shoes every year. Period. Shoes, every year. He would choose them himself without her counsel, and every year those shoes would be sturdy enough to last forever if her feet hadn't been growing. They were ugly enough to ruin a girls chances at life. She hated them, of course, and we disliked him for what the gift did to her. Christmas after Christmas. That, too, taught me to hedge truth at Christmas. I would tell her they were okay, cute, neat, great, or whatever the vernacular was of the year. And I always hoped against hope that it would help.

Then there was the girl who didn't even get a gift as grand as shoes. This family was the hardest hit in the Depression, and an apron from the girl's aunt to wear over her "clean-up" dress was a treasure to her. But she couldn't admit it. As we neared her house she'd begin talking grandly about how she had already put away all her gifts. There was no point in even going to her house, she'd insist. But everybody else persisted just the same.

That year I suggested, "Let's go to your house last." Maybe by then most of us would have to be on our way home and could skip her pain.

I loved this friend with a protective passion and gave her the best gift on my list—Evening in Paris in its midnight-blue bottle fitted into a special gift box. It came from Kresses on Third South, emporium of joy for kids from the Hill.

She always asked me what I wanted, and I'd lie each time and say the only thing I wanted was a jar of her mom's applesauce. And that's what she gave me, ribbon tied.

I think of that applesauce each canning season now, wondering why my own efforts never taste like the memory.

One Christmas I was sick but I also was suffering puppy-love pangs. My self-pity was disgusting. Late in the day the object of my puppy-love affection showed up by my bed with a little spaniel-puppy toy his mother had made from white shetland yarn. It was softly stuffed, button eyed, and crepe bottomed: a treasure forever.

"It's funny!" I struggled to laugh before I cried. For that toy from that boy was the most beautiful gift I had ever had. The one thing I really liked and I couldn't tell the truth about how much it meant to me!

And he lied back. "Oh, it's nothing!" But that comment didn't shadow the pride in his eyes. For he'd given to please, and I'd received it in the same spirit. And we both knew it no matter what was uttered. That's the wonder of Christmas.

Over the years I have been ill many a Christmas, for one reason or another, and three times I was hospitalized during the season of joy.

The first time, I was seventeen.

Carolers had long since sung and gone. Visitors had presented their poinsettias and returned to their own celebrations. The doctor pagings came over the speaker so softly now that only the night nurse could discern the details. The whole hospital was tuned way down to its customary night pattern.

Only it wasn't a customary night. It was Christmas Eve, and I was trapped there after surgery in a world dedicated to the grim realities of living and dying.

I was too young to die.

But was it living to be so lonely? I was homesick for my own bed, family, and familiar festivities in this most important, beloved, shining season.

One is always the child at Christmas, but my current situation nurtured only immaturity. I wailed and wallowed in self-pity.

That didn't help.

I pressed my eyes tight against the distractions of flashes flickering from the emergency-call-board out in the hall and pretended I was home, waiting for morning.

That didn't help, either. Christmas Eve is usually a restless night with much tossing and turning, giving in to wild speculation about Santa's plans.

I couldn't even turn over now. All I could do was move my arms.

As quickly as the thought crossed my mind, action followed. I clenched my fist and pushed with all my might against the wall behind my head, sending my wheeled hospital bed scooting out from the corner over to a fine place right before the window.

What joy!

No Bethlehem looked more welcome to the wise men than Salt Lake City's mid-avenues looked to me that night. Out there was Christmas.

This was an unfamiliar neighborhood, but the preparations were the same: tree lights still on in many front rooms; a dim bulb marking Santa's workshop in an attic, a basement, a storage porch, or garage; dark stretches in between where little ones wrestled with temptation to peek and did their own restless tossing and turning, their own kind of sweet suffering.

All those people beyond my hospital world excitedly going through the rituals of Christmas just as we did at our house! And all the bright dawnings that would follow. . . . I was amazed at my new, broader perspective.

I stretched my sore body for a better view. I heaped my heart into those houses with the lights still shining so far after midnight. I sighed a nice sigh. I didn't feel lonely anymore. People out there were making Christmas happen.

Suddenly certain yearnings stirred in me. I had always been such a taker — sleepless at Christmas wondering what I would get. But out there were people sleepless with the preparation of giving.

When the night nurse came in on her routine rounds, she was irate because my bed was out of position.

"Teenagers! Bah! Humbug!" she exclaimed.

"But it's Christmas out there." I feebly explained, as she pushed my bed back to its corner. "I need it to be Christmas in here."

Then I begged her to do a favor for me in the silence of the night. I had a table-sized Christmas tree that friends had brought. It was my only corner of Christmas and I loved it. But now I could use it well. I had something to give. Together we tore the signatures off of my Christmas cards and tucked the delightful pictures among the branches.

The night nurse smiled as she carried my perky tree down the hall as a Christmas surprise to the child from out of town.

And I settled down at last for a long Christmas nap.

The years passed, each with its shining season. I love every Christian, pagan, commercial, sentimental, underplanned, overdone aspect of Christmas. I love the legends, the myths, and the tender truth of its beginning as recorded in sacred writ.

Our young family was dedicated to the celebration in the fullest sense. We decked the halls with boughs of chains made from the faded green and red of school art paper. We tossed tinsel toward the tree and it fell to earth on the carpet, the hassock, the candlesticks. We sang the carols, every verse of every one. Our own nativity play was at once pitiful and charming. A birthday cake for baby Jesus was solemnly candled and joyfully cut. And we capped the celebration reading from Luke on Christmas Eve and unwrapped Christmas surprise-balls Christmas night.

Every Christmas it was the same wonderful sameness.

Yet every Christmas was different, too. It snowed or it didn't. The made-at-school clay handprint cracked or it didn't.

Someone had measles or miraculously all were well at once. The tree was pulled over by the newest toddler or it somehow survived. But it was Christmas and we didn't let anything spoil the feel of it.

For the Christmas of 1951 we did it all again. Finally, Santa had come in the still of the night, and in the chill of the dawn our own destroying angels had descended upon their gifts. It was an all-day exercise in the futility of organization. How do you organize who is going to want which toy when? The house qualified as a disaster area.

And I was in labor!

Surely the baby wouldn't come this early and ruin our Christmas day, I silently protested. Surely not.

Just as surely as I considered the situation, I learned the lesson that I was not in charge of such sacred happenings on any level. For that Christmas season, the days were accomplished that I should be delivered and bring forth our fifth-born child. The hospital staff had been reduced to holiday proportions, and someone accused us of not having planned very well.

How could our planning match the will of God anyway? Why, with his timing, I was turned into a Mary for a time. For unto us a child was born that forever after has added wonder to our celebration. No season before had matched that one, as I cradled her close to my heart and wondered and wept that Mary could survive seeing her Christmas child crucified on a cross.

We have celebrated Christmas with greater reverence since Holly's birth. Artwork of the holy family took precedence over meaningless decor. The children learned the difference between the Savior and Santa Claus, and our own Christmas baby grew and waxed strong in spirit, reminding us again and again of the real reason for the celebration.

Christmas ruined? No. Christmas forever after blessed, for a baby born at this season is a glorious gift. We named ours Holly, a name which stood, the record said, for happiness. And since she was born, it stands for blessing.

9

Christmas Because
of Christ

"Our Lord Jesus, that great Shepherd"
— *Hebrews 13:20*

"This is our God; we have waited for him"
— *Isaiah 25:9*

9

Christmas Because of Christ

 Without the Lord Jesus Christ the special essence that *is* Christmas would be lacking! Whatever we feel of spirit, love, lift, and inimitable joy at Christmas (or any other time of the year!) is because his Spirit touches us, not because the Christian world has declared December twenty-fifth as the time to celebrate his birth, as a holy day or holiday.

The occasion of Christmas itself is not as vital as the moment of truth that can come to each of us that Christ was born under absolutely unique circumstances and for a wise purpose which all the rest of his life fulfilled, and that he is who he is —our Savior, our Leader, the Creator of this world, Heaven's Gatekeeper, Prince of Peace, our Mighty and Good Friend! He is that great shepherd. He is the Son of God!

I know this. I have learned wonderful truths about the Savior by studying the scriptures. I have been to Bethlehem, Jerusalem, Canaan, Bethany, and to Galilee, Gethsemane, Golgotha, and the Garden Tomb where prophets have declared that Christ was risen following the crucifixion.

I have read Milton. I have read historical works concerning Christ. Around the world, and with great emotion, I have viewed religious art about the Savior, and have thrilled at music written in praise to him. I have also sung the simple, moving hymns to worship him.

I have considered the Savior's creation of the world and marveled at plant and animal life on all levels and in their infinite variety. What beauty there is, as well as remarkable utility in the elements, weather, mountains, sun, and night sky.

Intellectually I know that Jesus is the Son of God our Heavenly Father, and our Master.

I have gathered stories about ancient times and our own day, of his miracles with people—healings, comfortings, liftings, protectings, guidings, sustainings, inspirings, chastenings, forgivings, enhancings. I have witnessed miracles in my own life. I have counted my many blessings again and again because I have felt his spirit and have known his goodness. The fruits of my faith prove him for me.

Spiritually I know that God the Father, God the Son—known to us as Jesus Christ—and God the Holy Ghost are real; they operate in the affairs of this earth and its people—including you and me.

But I have done something else which I highly recommend to all: draw close to him and he will draw close to you! *Beyond the slightest doubt, you can know he lives and cares about you!*

I have been on my knees before Heavenly Father and in the name of Jesus Christ, and in humility and in hope and faith as we have been taught, I have poured out my heart expressing my gratitude and defining my needs. I have received answers to my prayers. Through the power of the Holy Ghost and in all humility, I testify that Christ lives! He lives! The worth of souls—yours and mine—is great to him.

Such a testimony, or absolute surety both intellectually and spiritually, makes all the difference to me and the great adventure that I, like you, am engaged in here on earth. It *is* the difference in how I view life, principles, blessings, relationships; the difference in how I hope, how I cope with the challenges and opportunities of life and of self. Meanwhile this knowledge influences our celebration of Christmas!

Old King Benjamin gave us a valuable clue to our celebration of life. He said: "Believe in God; believe that he is, and that he created all things, both in heaven and in earth; believe that he has all wisdom, and all power, both in heaven and in earth; believe that man doth not comprehend all the things which the Lord can comprehend." (Mosiah 4:9.)

Someone has suggested that there are many people who behave like kindergarten children at play, trying to spell God with the wrong blocks. At Christmas some people rush about buying this and that, or grieve because they cannot afford to, all the while wondering why they don't feel "the Christmas spirit."

President Marion G. Romney explains that as people actually become partakers of the Lord's divine nature, they acquire virtues that are perfected in the true and living God. Virtues like temperance, patience, brotherly kindness, and charity drive out selfishness, greed, lust, hate, and contentions. When this transformation occurs, peace, contentment, and joy naturally follow. "The almost universal prescript for peace today is 'return to God,' " said President Romney in an address at general conference of April 1970. " 'We must turn to God to find peace' is the cry of right-minded people throughout all the land. It is not because we do not know the remedy that peace escapes us. It is because we do not know the God to whom we must return."

Because we know the Lord and have full faith in him does not insure that we will be spared difficulties. But whether we have poverty or plenty, happiness or heartache in a certain season, circumstances are immaterial after all. What we know of Jesus and what we think of him influences the way we live our time on earth as well as the way we feel about Christmas. By being close to him, we can have our spirit of Christmas, our joy in celebrating his birth — we can appreciate his gifts to us, no matter what our circumstances are.

With God's help we can do away with all kinds of sin. But there is more . . . There is a wise observation from one of God's prophets of old that "wickedness never was happiness" (Alma 41:10). It is the flip side of the Ten Commandments, the Beatitudes, and the Articles of Faith.

Wickedness prohibits the Holy Spirit. Besides the usual definition, wickedness also is *not* treating others as they should be

treated. It is *not* being grateful for every small and sizable blessing. It is *not* loving God over Santa Claus.

It is *not* avoiding contention. Contention is of the devil and
is, of course, the absolute antithesis of the spirit of Christmas. I
have a friend who handles contention with a soft answer. She
has a firm Christmas rule that she recalls afresh with an embroidered pillow during the busy holidays: "No matter what a
child, an in-law, or my spouse does, I will keep the Christmas
spirit." Having declared that philosophy in public, she has
learned to handle stress by substituting laughter, a Christmas
jingle, a hymn, and quick hugs *before* a quarrel can happen.

With God's help we can deal with stress appropriately. Our
goal is to learn to find happiness whether or not we have stress;
whether we are accepted or rejected at work, school, church, in
social situations; whether or not we feel overworked and under-
paid; whether or not we are involved in miserable relationships;
whether or not we have youth and good health on our side!
Christmas reminds us that man is to have joy and the way has
been made clear for us to receive it, if we have the right blocks,
if we know the rules and the principles as well as the Master of
Happiness!

Again and again at this season the way seems easier, for we
feel his nearness because of who he is and what he is like.

That grand hymn "How Great Thou Art!" should be sung
as a Christmas carol, too:

> O Lord my God,
> when I in awesome wonder
> Consider all the worlds
> thy hands have made,
> I see the stars,
> I hear the rolling thunder,
> Thy pow'r throughout the universe displayed;
> Then sings my soul,
> my Savior God, to thee
> How great thou art!
> How great thou art!

Besides what he has created, he has given us so much. All
the bounties of life, loved ones, opportunities. Granted, some

days are better than others, some trials tougher than others. But
what an outpouring of blessings! What exquisite principles to
guide us to greater happiness!

Consider what he has said about love, the very root of
Christmas: "Thou shalt love the Lord thy God . . . and . . . thy
neighbour as thyself." (Matthew 22:37–39.) And we are to love
not only our neighbor but also enemies and strangers, all children of God!

An attractive, striving woman received an emergency call
to her critically ill daughter's bedside. It was Christmas Day and
travel options were limited. The only way she could get to her
daughter's home was by transcontinental bus.

This was a new experience. This woman lived comfortably
with a husband who sheltered her from unpleasantness as much
as possible. Waiting in a public bus depot was not on that list.
But wait she did, with the pitiful people of the world who had
heartbreaking problems like her own, or who had no place else
to be on Christmas Day: the "dregs of humanity" was the way
she described them. Drunks, homeless refugees, people with
lives out of control because of abusive substances or deviate
lifestyles.

The fact that it was Christmas Day and she was trying to be
a disciple of Christ made the experience the more significant to
her. She needed the blessings of God upon her daughter! She
wanted to qualify herself for such blessings. The first great qual-
ification was to love others as she loved herself.

"I didn't see one soul that I could even relate to," she explained. "These people weren't enemies, either; they were
people I simply did not understand. Love them? My brothers
and sisters? Children of God—these poor, pitiful, misguided
sinners and vagrants?"

She wondered if this sort of thing went on across the world
on Christmas Day. "How dreadful! How horrible! Christ was
born to solve these kinds of situations in life," she rehearsed in
her own mind. This was a severe test in the name of Christmas
and of him whose birthday she had been celebrating until the
call came from her son-in-law. Suddenly she admitted to a great
weakness in herself. She didn't know how to handle this situation. She didn't even want to sit on the bus next to people like

this, let alone feel love for them in her heart! But the test . . . the test! Her need of blessings for her own daughter!

In the moment of self-realization in contemplating Christ's ideals for living, she bowed her head in silent prayer. She pleaded for help, for forgiveness for arrogance and weakness. She prayed, too, for guidance for appropriate action on her part. She begged for strength, for the will to behave as Christ would have her behave. Silent prayer finished, she sat waiting, listening, reaching for spiritual confirmation that her prayers had been heard.

Her reverie was disturbed by a touch on her sleeve. She looked up into the searching eyes of a young mother with little ones clinging to her coat and a baby in her arms, a backpack and diaper bag adding to her burden.

"Could you help me, please?" asked the young mother. "You seem a nice sort of person that I could trust. Could you hold my baby and watch these things so I can take these toddlers to the restroom! We've been trying to get to my husband's family for Christmas and have missed connections and everything. It has been so awful. They're so tired and . . . "

The baby was shifted from the weary young mother to the well-groomed grandmother who reached out her arms to help.

"All the time I held that baby, I thought of Christmas . . . of Mary and the baby Jesus . . . of Santa Claus in abundance in the homes of people I knew . . . of the grown Christ who waxed strong and brought such goodness into the world. And I thought of myself and my need to grow and wax wonderful!" she explained. "Yes, I was to love them. I was to help them, to generate goodwill even if it were only with a smile and a few coins for tired children, only with being as useful as I could. And I did that all the rest of the day in that bus stop and across the many miles into the night before I arrived at the city where our daughter lived."

It was her most unusual Christmas, the celebration being an adventure in needing and helping. It was also her most memorable Christmas. The Spirit of the Lord filled her as she performed unselfish service; as she taught simple truths about the real meaning of Christmas to her fellow passengers as occasion permitted; as she listened to tragic tales of heartbreak, bad luck, and ill health, comforting as she could.

But there was more: she witnessed the stricken and deprived helping each other. People downwind in life could still be touched by the spirit of caring. The crowning moment for this woman of means and high station in God's Church came at bus-boarding time. A man of dubious lifestyle, if clothes and the smell of body and breath were any indication, helped her load her baggage on board, reverently calling her "Mother." Her laughter as she tells the story doesn't hide the dew in her eyes.

By the time she had arrived at the hospital, she entered the trauma of her daughter's life not selfishly frantic but mellowed. She was grateful and confident that Jesus cared, that he blessed as was best for his children, that he could use all kinds of people to do his work, especially at Christmastime.

We are showered with the beauty of the world, with intriguing and rewarding relationships and friendships, with joy in watching unique personalities unfold in our loved ones, with the guiding spirit of teachers, with models for life among leaders and prophets. And, oh yes, health, comfort like mankind has never known, protection of person and property, adventures, challenges. He gives us strength to resist temptations, purpose in stretching mind and heart, faith-bolstering experiences.

And he gave his life for us. We feel his love for us and it is an incredible blessing. The spirit of truth in a man leads to righteousness. Righteousness leads to happiness.

However, then, in all this world of plenty is there yet celebration enough for someone to whom we owe so much? How can we make Christmas marvelous enough to mark the birth of the "Lamb of God . . . the Son of the Eternal Father?" (1 Nephi 13:40.)

At this Christmas season, we remember that the Lord loves us as he obviously loved the young woman speaking at the Christmas program, and the only gift we can give him in return, the only way we can make celebration sufficient to our blessings from him, is to love others and to do his will in bringing them joy and direction.

There is a long-remembered bit of wisdom, by some forgotten genius with whom I agree and whom I frequently quote: "for the withholding of love is the negation of the spirit of Christ, the proof that we never knew him, that for us he lived in vain. It means that he suggested nothing in all our thoughts, that he inspired nothing in all our lives, that we were not once near enough to him to be seized with the spell of his compassion for the world."

Without having Christlike love as part of our celebrating, Christmas after Christmas, relationship following relationship would come and then, disappointingly, dwindle.

I received a letter from an irate woman who felt that her sister and brother-in-law had cheated her family out of their share of an inheritance. I did not know this woman, nor did she really know me, for she concluded her outburst with this suggestion written in capital letters: "Why don't you call them on a mission so they can get out of our hair and maybe even learn what followers of Christ ought to be like!"

That is an ultimate irony, isn't it?

The spirit of Christmas is the spirit of Christ, and the season gives us the *comfortable excuse*, which sometimes we seem to need, for bringing peace into our relationships. The real business of Christmas is to courageously reconcile differences; to heal wounds of the heart; to overcome quarrels with relatives, business associates, neighbors, and friends; and to endure silently if that's what is required.

It is tending the stroke victim with respect and tenderness as well as patience, for as long as it takes!

It is paying tithes and offerings quickly, happily, and with gratitude that the work of the Lord may move forward.

It is remembering that the birth of Jesus introduced mercy, repentance, hope, and love into the world, and that our part is to find ways to implement these virtues into daily living.

It is quietly doing what needs to be done, in the name of Jesus Christ, without looking for credit or praise.

One women's leader has *counted* and listed 2300 meals that she prepared for families who gathered after the 2300 funerals! Remarkable! Even with ever-ready helpers, that is some record. But isn't the spirit of Christ doing and *not* counting?

None of us is perfect, yet. We learn and do, a step and a principle at a time. The blessing of Christmas is to fill us with determination to make the next year better. President George Q. Cannon wrote, "If any of us are imperfect, it is our duty to pray for the gift that will make us perfect. Have I imperfections?

I am full of them. What is my duty? To pray to God to give me the gifts that will correct these imperfections. If I am an angry man, it is my duty to pray for charity, which suffereth long and is kind. Am I an envious man? It is my duty to seek for charity, which envieth not. So with all the gifts of the gospel. They are intended for this purpose. No [one] ought to say, 'Oh, I cannot help this; it is my nature.' He is not justified in it, for the reason that God had promised to give strength to correct these things and to give gifts that will eradicate them."

Christmas is a time to teach the truth through the symbols and stories of the season. We can look for ways to make our traditions valuable for all aspects of life.

I am thinking of the very first Christmas crèche we bought. The children were small, and so was our bank account, but from the variety store we managed to purchase an adequate manger with rather lovely figures for the scene, as well as the animals, a star, and an angel with a hood on its back to hold it to the roof of the manger just in front of the Christmas star. They were of pastel-colored wax.

We took the pieces from the store container and when we came to the angel, I was worried. This angel had wings! Naturally, the children were interested in this.

"This angel looks like a person," said Carla. "Do people have wings when they die?" Nana Cannon had just died, and the children were very interested in what happened to dead people.

That did it. This was a teaching moment and the gospel was to be explained as accurately as possible to these eager, precious children lent to us for a season on earth.

"No, they do not," I answered. "Whoever made these figures just didn't understand, so he put wings on as a way to show that angels are different from people. They can go where they want to—even to earth when they are sent by Heavenly Father." As I struggled to explain, the excitement over our new nativity set suddenly diminished, tarnished by an inaccurate angel!

"Well," said Carla, "if Nana doesn't have wings, this angel shouldn't have wings either."

"Then we will remove them," I said bravely. And I used a

paring knife to carve away the angel's wings. When the task was finished and we mounted the angel on her perch, Carla said, "We did a good deed, didn't we? We fixed that angel better."

Better, maybe, certainly not prettier. But butchered or not, that angel was a teaching aid and Christmas was no time to compromise with God's truth.

For years after the incident we'd laugh when we'd take that scarred angel from its wrappings for another holiday appearance. Growing children never forgot the lesson and all the neighbors who visited during the season had the lesson explained to them, too.

As we come to know the truth about angels as well as about the Christ child, our Christmas spirit will be more constant, vital, lasting, encompassing, and motivating.

People who have visited the Church of the Nativity in Bethlehem have been disappointed with the confusion in the long hall leading to the low entrance over the cave, where many believe Christ actually was born. There is a strange mix of numerous baubles, bangles, lanterns, and bells, all dusty and dingy hanging from the high ceiling. There is the door to the sacred niche where a famous oil painting of the Nativity marks the manger. That door is so small that only a child can enter without squatting through.

Stooping through that door is symbolic, some say, of the day when "every knee should bow . . . every tongue should confess that Jesus Christ is the Lord." (Philippians 2:10–11.)

All of which calls to mind the old Christmas verse, "Let not our hearts be busy inns that have no room for thee." Instead, may we take a moment at Christmas to determine that we will love God with all our heart, might, mind, and strength, and in the name of Jesus Christ serve him. Now, after all and all, what we think of Jesus also influences the way we celebrate Christmas.

Envoi

"May joy come from God above
To all those who Christmas love."
(From a thirteenth-century carol)

And may each of us remember him,
The best of all friends,
Whose birthday we celebrate as Christmas.
And may each of us remember himself,
As a child of God, too.
And may each of us treasure the best of our times —
Endless Christmases —
And all because of him.

May Love and joy abide with you;

May All Good guide you ever.

May gladness live in all you do

May sweet Hope fail you never.